AF535109

EARLIER THAN PLANNED

KRISTILYN WISEMAN

EARLIER THAN PLANNED

TRUSTING IN THE DIVINITY OF YOUR MISSION CALL AND RELEASE

Covenant Communications, Inc.

Cover images: *Man with Suitcase* © Yuri_Arcurs, courtesy of istock.com and *Woman with Suitcase* © Leolintang, courtesy of istock.com.

Cover design copyright © 2021 by Covenant Communications, Inc.

Published by Covenant Communications, Inc.
American Fork, Utah
First published as an ebook titled *Accepting Your Call to Come Home: A Message of Hope for Early-Released Missionaries*

Copyright © 2018 by Kristilyn Wiseman
All rights reserved. No part of this book may be reproduced in any format or in any medium without the written permission of the publisher, Covenant Communications, Inc., P.O. Box 416, American Fork, UT 84003. This work is not an official publication of The Church of Jesus Christ of Latter-day Saints. The views expressed within this work are the sole responsibility of the author and do not necessarily reflect the position of The Church of Jesus Christ of Latter-day Saints, Covenant Communications, Inc., or any other entity.

This material is neither made, provided, approved, nor endorsed by Intellectual Reserve, Inc. or The Church of Jesus Christ of Latter-day Saints. Any content or opinions expressed, implied or included in or with the material are solely those of the owner and not those of Intellectual Reserve, Inc. or The Church of Jesus Christ of Latter-day Saints.

Printed in the United States of America
First Printing: April 2021

27 26 25 24 23 22 21 10 9 8 7 6 5 4 3 2 1

ISBN 978-1-52441-810-6

To all returned missionaries who took their name tags off sooner than anticipated.
The Lord knows your service.

TESTIMONIALS

Increased numbers of missionaries have been accompanied by increased numbers returning home early. Reasons vary as much as each individual living through this difficult experience, but this wonderful and timely book offers real help. I love and admire Kristilyn and her fellow authors who have shared their journeys so openly and honestly. Their paths have been different, but each path has led to a better understanding of the Lord, His work, and His grace. These returned missionaries' insights can help all of us see the big picture, feel hope, and recognize God's hand in our lives.

—Brad Wilcox, Author of *The Continuous Atonement* and *Changed through His Grace*

I have witnessed the personal devastation of those close to me who could not fulfill their desire to serve a mission because of sheer physical inability. This book needs to be shared throughout the Church so that others may feel the love and encouragement that Kristilyn and these other early-released missionaries finally gained. Their messages show why every single person is needed in God's kingdom—no matter where, how, or when, every contribution is noted, counted, and treasured. This is a must read for anyone who has felt the heartache of returning early.

—Sharlene Wells, Former Miss America

ACKNOWLEDGMENTS

Thank you to my husband for loving me unconditionally; my parents for advocating for me and helping me do what I could not finish alone; my family for supporting me both on and off the mission; my companions for never complaining; each of the contributors for willingly reliving difficult experiences in order to help others in similar situations; Jessica Naval for sharing her photography talent; Sharlene Wells Hawkes and Brad Wilcox for mentoring and offering guidance throughout the various stages of this project; and my editor, Kami Hancock, and Covenant Communications for giving us the opportunity to share our testimonies of Christ through our personal experiences.

TABLE OF CONTENTS

FOREWORD

Beloved Returned Missionary:

This book has been written for you as you return home early from your mission. Whatever the reason your mission has been cut short, this early return was never part of your plan or expectation. When you looked forward to your mission—dreamed of your mission—this return wasn't at all part of what you envisioned. Nor do we anticipate that things will be easy for you during this transition. For you who have prepared to serve the Lord as full-time missionaries with all your heart, might, mind, and strength (see D&C 4:2), the weeks and months ahead may count as among the greatest challenges you have yet faced. Some of you reading this book will eventually return to the field to serve as full-time missionaries; others, through no fault of your own and contrary to every faithful and worthy desire of your heart, will not. While your individual circumstances will vary, this book has been prepared with great love and admiration to let you know how very much your Father in Heaven loves you and appreciates your service as a full-time missionary.

The Lord has promised, "I have heard thy prayer, I have seen thy tears: behold, I will heal thee" (2 Kings 20:5). We testify to you that the Lord truly does hear your prayers (and those of countless others who are even now praying for you) and that He sees your tears, and He will indeed heal you, if you will let Him. This healing will take different forms, however, and might be different from your expectations. Some of you will be healed physically or emotionally, in short order. Others will fully recover, but over a longer period of time. In some cases, however, physical or emotional maladies—including the deep and very real pain initiated by your early return—will persist, and your healing will be of a very different nature (see Psalm 147:3, Luke 4:18).

You may feel lost or forgotten during this process. We assure you that you are not forgotten (see 1 Ne. 21:14, Luke 12:6), and we promise that as you remain true to the covenants you have made, the Lord will help you find your way through the challenges that lie ahead of you. He knows you, and He has a plan for you. He who notices the falling of a sparrow surely remembers those who have served faithfully as divinely called missionaries, regardless of the length of that service.

Some of you who read this will eventually return to full-time missionary service, but many of you will not. Heavenly Father has different plans for you at this time in your life and has called you elsewhere for purposes known to Him. In some instances, this may be the only way He can call you to a different situation at this time in your life, as difficult as returning home early may seem right now.

Your mission is no less complete or valued when it is cut short by illness or global pandemic or other causes through no fault of your own. Those who respond to the call of the Savior with full purpose of heart, for however long the calling is extended to them, are equal in the eyes of the Lord, for they are His. Matthew 20:10–14 teaches this important lesson as follows:

> But when the first came, they supposed that they should have received more; and they likewise received every man a penny. And when they had received it, they murmured against the goodman of the house, [s]aying, These last have wrought but one hour, and thou hast made them equal unto us, which have borne the burden and heat of the day. But he answered one of them, and said, Friend, I do thee no wrong: didst not thou agree with me for a penny? Take that thine is, and go thy way: I will give unto this last, even as unto thee.

You can still serve Heavenly Father in many ways. He loves you and will watch over you as you experience this unexpected change of calling. Be assured that He needs you no less than He did previously, that He loves you no less than He did previously, and that His plan for you has not lessened or diminished in any way. There may in fact come a day when you will fully understand how your current situation and trials fit ever lovingly into that plan for you. Fear not and be comforted, for your prayers are heard (see Luke 1:13); God is watching over you, and He will never forsake you (see Matt. 27:46, Mark 15:34). The Source of all callings is overseeing yours, even now, and He will continue to do so in the future as you continue to have desires to serve (see D&C 4:3).

As you pray and counsel with your parents and leaders, you will be led in the paths He would have you walk, and you will be blessed with opportunities to serve and to share the gospel. Consider the words of President Thomas S.

Monson: "As you plan with purpose your [life], remember that your missionary opportunities are not restricted to the period of a formal call."[1]

This book contains the first-hand accounts of several missionaries, both elders and sisters, who have returned home from their missions for reasons beyond their control. It shares the heartache and pain and loneliness each went through and recounts how each overcame these trials and ultimately found new hope and renewed direction through the healing power of the Atonement of Jesus Christ. These are their own stories, told in their own words, edited only for length and clarity. Each of these missionaries wrote their stories with you in mind so that they might reach out to you with reassurance and encouragement that not only can you get through this unexpected challenge but you can also be strengthened and truly be a tool in the Master's hand as He heals you and guides you in His own way.

One final note: On December 17, 2010, the city of Provo, Utah, awoke to tragic news: the historic Provo Tabernacle—an important and distinguished building in that community—was engulfed in flames. The insides of the building were largely destroyed, and the roof collapsed in the blaze. When the fire was extinguished, the building was initially considered a total loss. At the time, many people wondered how such a terrible thing could happen to such a wonderful, sacred building. Many asked, "How could God have allowed this terrible tragedy to happen to such a beautiful dedicated building?" But out of the ashes of that terrible fire eventually arose, through time and effort, a temple of God, a house of the Lord—a building even more sacred and dedicated to higher purposes than what would have been possible had that fire never happened. Such are the ways and designs of the Master Architect.

"Know ye not that ye [also] are the temple of God . . . ? . . . The temple of God is holy, *which temple ye are*" (1 Cor. 3:16–17; emphasis added). Be of good courage, and trust in Him; He is watching over you and will continue to do so. Just as He was able to cause a beautiful and holy temple to be brought forth from the devastation of the Provo Tabernacle fire, so He can and will make of you something better and holier and more pure if you will allow Him to do so. "Trust in [Him] with all thine heart; and lean not unto thine own understanding. In all thy ways acknowledge him, and he shall direct thy paths" (Prov. 3:5–6).

Thank you so much for your consecrated service and desires to serve. May Heavenly Father's blessings ever be with you, and may you come to gain the sweet and healing assurance that He has accepted of your offering (see D&C 124:49).

—Bruce Gelder, Mission Presidency Counselor

---

1 Thomas S. Monson, "Come, All Ye Sons of God," *Ensign*, May 2013, 67.

INTRODUCTION

Our purpose in writing this book is not to complain or to receive pity, praise, or attention. While we don't know exactly what each early-returned missionary feels, our own journeys allow us to relate to the soul-encompassing sting caused from an unexpected release in a way otherwise impossible. Our hope is that missionaries returning home sooner than planned might find comfort and love in the words, feelings, stories, and testimonies we share.

We wish to acknowledge that we too felt anger, weakness, guilt, betrayal, loss, and humiliation. We each experienced attacks by Satan to weaken us, yet we found that the gospel and the unconditional love of Heavenly Father empowers individuals to minimize the adversary's influence in our lives. Moreover, we wish to affirm the eternal worth of your mission, regardless of length or cause of release, and offer hope during the healing process. Our aim is to reach out to all whose physical and mental health or other personal circumstances can cause peril to their spiritual health and to help them see that these experiences can, by contrast, steer them to come unto Christ.

We also realize that countless family members, friends, and Church leaders desire to serve early-returned missionaries but often do not understand the widespread range of emotional and spiritual distress they experience. May our journeys better enable them to love, support, and value those struggling with their early return.

As we have reflected, often painfully and tearfully, on our own experiences to record for you here, we realized how much our understanding of the Savior's ever-outstretched hand has been magnified. Through His Atonement, we can find hope and peace, even and especially during our long, lonely days and nights. We are never alone. It is through Jesus Christ that we can triumph. He is the way. As we follow that way, we will find that we have great reason to rejoice.

We must cling to God's promise in the Doctrine and Covenants:

> And if it so be that you should labor all your days in crying repentance unto this people, and bring, save it be one soul unto me, how great shall be your joy with him in the kingdom of my Father! (D&C 18:15)

The promise is that your joy *shall* be great. Sometimes Heavenly Father gives us glimpses of the joy right away. Other times, we have to hold on to the promise. You labored with your whole soul to serve God. Your joy shall be great, even if, in the moment, it's not. Trust God. His promises are sure and eternal. God will teach you through still, quiet moments of revelation that He loves you and accepts your offering.

CHAPTER 1
AN INSPIRED RELEASE
BY KRISTILYN WISEMAN

"Be strong and of a good courage; be not afraid, neither be thou dismayed: for the Lord thy God is with thee whithersoever thou goest." (Joshua 1:9)

My biggest fear was that I wouldn't leave with my group. I was scared to be stuck at the missionary training center (MTC), the sickly girl who would burden another companionship. And once I finally got better, I'd probably need to fly to my mission—fly to *Asia*—by myself. I had no idea that just days later this option would seem like heaven compared to my new alternative.

Those weeks I spent sick at the MTC were some of the hardest weeks of my life. I was grateful I'd already been on my mission for nearly two months when I got sick so that my companions, district, teachers, zone, and branch presidency knew the *normal* me. There I was—a marathon runner—dizzy, with no energy whatsoever, and my body just ached. At times during computer language study I'd just sit staring at the screen trying to process any kind of information and then lean forward to rest my head in my hands. Most of the time others couldn't tell how sick I was simply by looking at me, so I knew it appeared I was just being lazy and apathetic.

To take the sting away, I would joke that I just did whatever I wanted—made up my own schedule, slept when I wanted, ate when I chose, and rarely went to class. But it wasn't funny. I hated it. I hated that I couldn't serve with my whole heart. I hated not knowing what was causing my illness. And most of all I hated that I couldn't do anything about it. As time progressed, the doctors continued to run tests. I spent most days in the sick bay at the MTC health office, or my *daycare* as my companions and I jokingly referred to it. My selfless companions then took turns in the evenings missing class to babysit me.

One week before my scheduled flight to Korea, I started feeling a little better. I had written to my family that I would probably be well enough to go to Korea on time with my zone.

We had our travel plans to fly out the following Monday and we could almost taste the Korean air. Then the doctor threw me the curveball. I wouldn't get my latest test results until Tuesday, the day after the flight, and I doubted they'd let me out of the country without the test results that could hopefully provide answers as to why I was so sick. Thoughts raced through my mind. *I know I'm supposed to go to Korea. Everyone's been praying and fasting for me. Even if my faith isn't enough, surely Heavenly Father would listen to the prayers of all these other missionaries, my mission presidency, and my family. He can heal me. He's a God of miracles, and He can heal me.*

I tearfully told my companions, "Man, Satan really doesn't want me to go to Korea. Things just keep coming up to try to stop me." The instant the words came out of my mouth, I had a distinct impression from the Holy Ghost by way of words in my mind: *Maybe Heavenly Father doesn't want you to go to Korea.* It was a foreign thought. Why would God not want me to go to my mission field? Wasn't the answer to just have faith that Heavenly Father would heal me? Miraculous mission stories always included faith and healing, right? Confusion clouded my already foggy mind.

At the temple with my zone, I felt very distinctly that my sickness would cause me to go home. The impression completely caught me off guard, and I questioned if it came from God or was my own thought. *I don't want to go home. Am I that sick? I don't need to go home. What does Heavenly Father want from me?* I felt the love from my companions, who were sitting next to me. They had become two of my closest friends in a short couple of months. Seeing the faces of the elders and sisters from Korea whom I had grown to love, I suddenly realized that if I went home, I might never serve with them in Korea or see them again in this life.

I didn't even know what to pray for now. So much hope and gratitude had filled my prayers the past few days because of my seemingly miraculous recovery. That night I tearfully knelt at the side of my bed and prayed, telling Heavenly Father how confused I was. I loved my mission and was so grateful that I was getting better. I didn't want to go home—I wanted so badly to go to Korea, but I didn't know what Heavenly Father wanted. I begged Heavenly Father over and over to let me stay on my mission. Ultimately, however, I prayed that my body would do what it needed to in order for me to do God's will.

Wednesday morning I woke up as sick as ever. Recognizing that this was likely the answer to my prayer, I cried to Heavenly Father, sobbing the only words that would come: *I'm here, I'm here*—that is, I was at the MTC, set apart as a missionary, ready and *wanting* to go to Korea in five days. Why would He take me from such a good, righteous thing? Thursday came with no improvements in my health. I was devastated to find out that the very next morning they were sending me home. I had at least hoped to stay for a few days to say goodbye to my MTC leaders and especially to join in singing the traditional "Arirang" Korean folksong with missionaries in my zone before the other missionaries flew to Korea.

The first time I wore a missionary tag off MTC grounds wasn't supposed to be on my flight home. But even though it was, I couldn't talk to people and share my testimony. I was just too weak and disheartened. I took breaks on benches while walking through the airports in order to regain energy and spent both flights trying not to throw up or pass out. The plane ride magnified the dizziness, and the fatigue was almost more than I could handle.

In the airport, some members of the Church excitedly wanted to know if I was leaving for my mission field or returning home after serving my mission. I painfully explained that I was going home temporarily for health reasons. Saying it out loud made my nightmare a reality. My faith-led dreams felt like they'd gotten thrown in the dumpster and were laughing in my face. Although I figured the strangers probably wouldn't have a second thought about my situation, I was heartbroken and embarrassed. I guiltily brushed my long hair over my name tag to prevent further questions.

I'd be getting released as a full-time missionary that night. The plan was for me to fly to Korea as soon as I was healthy, which doctors predicted would be just a few weeks. However, I felt in my heart I was likely home for good. How quickly this dream had come and gone. It seemed my world was spinning around me in a nauseating combination of my sickness and emotions.

Like every other missionary in the MTC, I had been positive that my mission was the very best mission in the world and that I could and would make a difference. I sang "Called to Serve" with thousands of missionaries, and I meant every word. I hoped and dreamed about the people I would teach. About the very individuals I had been promised needed me at this particular time. And then I found out it wasn't for me. I didn't know why. But all of a sudden I was home and that wasn't my life any more.

I've heard people say that missionaries whose missions are cut short by death go straight to the Celestial Kingdom because they were completely spending their lives in labors of love, working continuously to build God's kingdom on earth. They become heroes when they are called in this way to their heavenly home, and rightly so.

It's not the same when you're called back to your earthly home.

What I desperately craved was the validation normal returned missionaries received. All I really wanted was for people to wrap their arms around me in total love and welcome me home. I wanted people to tell me I had done a good job. I wished that someone—anyone—would ask me how my mission was. I *wanted* to tell people about the life-changing experiences I'd had. I *wanted* to show off the Korean I'd learned, even as limited as it was. I *wanted* people to ask to see pictures and hear stories.

But the requests rarely came. And I certainly wasn't going to share something so close to my heart when others didn't seem to care about it. I knew most people simply didn't know what to say or were trying to avoid asking questions that could potentially make me feel uncomfortable, but their silence seemed to be a testament that my mission didn't matter and that no one cared about anything I had done. I ached for any kind of outside support or affirmation.

Every conversation reminded me I was at home and not in Korea. I hated answering people's questions about what kind of sickness I did or didn't have. I didn't want suggestions on what I should or shouldn't do for my body. *That's what doctors are for,* I thought. And I'd been seeing my fair share of them recently. I was tired of feeling like I'd *become* the illness. The only questions I seemed to ever answer were about my health and when I could go back on my mission. Well-meaning people seemed to forget about *me*. They seemed to forget I was hurting and alone and confused. That I missed my mission more than I had words to say and that the thought of never returning to it scared me even more than the very real possibility that I might have a serious health problem.

Several people told me about missionaries they knew who had gotten sick but had miraculously gotten better through prayers and fasting. While I appreciated their attempts to find some common ground with me, all I could really hear was that I should have prayed harder and fasted more. Or at least not given up so easily. No one cheers for the person who gives up, especially when the task is God-given.

I was mortified when people generalized my exhaustion and said things like, "Oh yeah, you've always loved sleeping. Missionary work definitely makes you tired." Pity comments. I felt betrayed when, oblivious to my deeper health issues, they so quickly assumed I would just give up something so dear to my heart because I would rather sleep. I cringed every time someone responded to me after I said I came home early for being sick with, "Oh, were you homesick?" It felt like an attack on every part of me that I held dear: my testimony, dedication, determination, the gospel, and my entire sense of identity and self-worth. Later on, thoughtless remarks like, "Oh, so you didn't really serve?" or "So, you just served a little bit?" weren't intended to hurt as much as they did.

They didn't know I dreaded then—and still do to this day—answering the typically uncomplicated question of, "Did you serve a mission?" I hated that there was no simple answer because once I said yes, they'd ask where and I couldn't just say Korea and leave it at that. People expect you to have actually been to the location you say your mission was in. Overall, people just didn't know how much I loved my mission.

The minute I got home, all I really wanted was to be close to Korea, even if that meant through my meager attempts to create my own Korea in Iowa. I prayed in Korean and tried teaching my family basic Korean phrases. I'd practice the language by reciting Joseph Smith's first vision in my head and listening to conference talks in Korean even though the level of my language understanding only allowed me to pick out handfuls of vocabulary words rather than complete ideas or even sentences. I just craved hearing the beautiful Korean language I'd been surrounded by for the past few months.

I concluded that even if I couldn't be in Korea myself, I could maybe help the work progress in some way by encouraging those whom I loved so much who were serving there. With dedication, I wrote my companions letters once a week and rotated writing other missionaries in my zone. Each day I prayed personally for every missionary in my zone whose name I could remember.

The guilt began with all the little things—my unused plane ticket to Korea, expensive doctors' visits and tests, stress placed on my family, money people had chipped in to help with the cost of my mission, the letters I'd received as a missionary with words, which now haunted me, about how proud they were of me. I felt like a failure every time I looked at my mission shoes, especially the ones I'd been saving to wear in Korea. *Good* missionaries are supposed to come back with worn-out shoes, not barely worn shoes.

Although my missionary release was labeled an honorable one, it didn't feel like it. I felt like I had sinned. Except with this sin, I didn't know how to change it or how to make up for what I had done wrong. I told God I'd serve Him in Korea for eighteen months. I *had* tried to complete my mission. But when everything added up, I hadn't. I felt like I had lied to God. And there wasn't anything honorable about that.

In reality, I had no reason to feel at fault. My body had simply grown too weak. Logically, I knew I could hold my head high with confidence that I'd served God during my mission with my whole heart and not just "a little bit."

But Satan's lies intertwined with my own thoughts so that I couldn't tell what was real and what wasn't. I didn't understand why these emotions trumped the facts.

Maybe there would have been less room for Satan's lies to get in my head if I had been out busy doing things—as most people recommend for newly returned missionaries. But there was none of that for me. The adversary had plenty of time and opportunity. My family and I joked that my life and my cat's life weren't much different: I slept most of the day, grazed on food when I was awake, rarely left the house, and waited for my parents to come home from work.

The highlight of my day was checking the mail for letters from Korea. While sick at the MTC, I felt encircled in the other missionaries' love and support. But now, they were living a completely new and different life, far from the steps of my front door. I lived for any connection to my mission, any confirmation that my mission was more than a dream and that someone remembered it and me.

Each day for weeks, I walked the fifty or so feet to my mailbox and back—a significant amount of exercise for my current condition, and typically the only time I left my house besides for doctors' appointments, an occasional visit to my brother's family, and attending portions of church. Each day for more than a month, I found nothing from Korea.

Although an overwhelming amount of love and support later flooded in from my companions, missionaries in my zone, and some missionaries in Korea whom I'd never even met, Satan used clever tactics during the delay of communication to drain my spirit by overflowing my lonely heart with convincing lies: *You mean nothing to them. Real missionaries have faith, and all those missionaries can see that you don't. They're busy actually serving God right now. Nobody has time for you anymore. Everyone's forgotten you. You are alone.*

I felt guilty for feeling so depressed. After all, so many people in the world had it a lot worse than I did. What was my problem? I got to sleep every day, hang out, watch movies, and have no obligations. But that was the problem. Almost everything I loved about life—mission or not—felt like it had been sucked away from me. For weeks that turned into months, I felt I had nothing to wake up to in the morning.

Several months after my release, I recorded in my journal, *So often I just feel worthless, misled, and broken. I feel like I did something horribly wrong to get so far off course. No one has any idea. I've been trying to use the Atonement [of Jesus Christ], but I just feel so stuck. I know things are in God's hands. It's just so hard finding and seeing my way. I have no idea why my world is as shaken up as it is. I never in a million years would have guessed this would be so hard.*

I felt betrayed by the entire situation. I had signed up to serve a mission, to serve God. And now, though by no fault of my own, I felt entirely unwanted by Him. My unused Korean visa and proselyting card served as physical reminders to me that during the very time I fought to feel God near me, I was supposed to be having what others refer to as the greatest spiritual experiences of my life.

It began to hurt too much to talk about my mission—and the loss of it—so conversations were quick and to the point. It was an unconscious act of self-defense. And it wasn't so much that I didn't want other people to know of my heartache; it was more that I didn't even understand the way I was feeling or why it was so hard. I had been home nearly ten months before I was able to begin to express any of my feelings, even to my parents.

I only shared brief glimpses of my difficulties with two close friends who had come home early themselves. Only a year before, I had tried to reassure one of them that coming home early because of illness was not her fault. Now the tables were turned. I knew she wouldn't judge me or get the wrong idea about the fact that I now found it difficult to read scriptures, that I tuned out at any church talk about missionary work, that I hated singing the missionary hymn "Called to Serve," and that I struggled speaking with my Father in Heaven through prayer. Emotional and spiritual vertigo clouded my sight with the warped self-image Satan so desperately wanted me to have, but the steady gaze of my friends led me to better see myself as the Savior does.

Somewhere in my heart, I *knew* Heavenly Father really did need me but just needed me somewhere else. At the same time, I got mad at myself for struggling with the transition of coming home as much as I did. After all, it didn't seem like it should be that hard—plan A got cancelled, so I should just move to plan B. But it wasn't that easy.

In every other trial I'd been through before, I was always strengthened by increased diligence in scripture study, temple attendance, and prayer. But I was at a loss for what to do when the divine resources I always trusted to heal pain were the very ones at the source of all the hurt.

My scriptures overflowed with notes and memories from my mission, including verses I'd marked about my purpose as a missionary and how Heavenly Father would help me learn the language and teach my Korean people. When I was finally well enough to attend the temple, the memory of my last session with my zone replayed in my mind—the memory of the prompting that I would go home—and that triggered memories of all the events and emotions that followed. And whenever I tried to sincerely open up to God in prayer, I found myself crying—not so much saying a prayer, but *feeling* one.

I just missed my Father in Heaven. Although it didn't logically make sense, I felt that I'd fallen from Him. Even though I was going through the motions of the things I knew were right, I felt spiritually dehydrated, like a thirsty runner who keeps drinking water but nothing seemed to be getting through to the body.

Despite the hole in my heart, Heavenly Father found ways to fill it. Friends, family, and neighbors reached out in love, reminding me that I was never alone. People of a variety of faiths who had never met me but had heard of my situation began praying for me. God used the kindness of others to show me that I would be all right. I didn't know how or when things would start getting better, but the Spirit reminded me over and over that they would. My heart would not always be empty. He whispered to me repeatedly that my mission mattered to God as well as those around me and that I should be grateful for the blessing I had of serving as His missionary during the time I did.

In my journal I wrote, *I don't know what's in store for me or my future. I can't change things now or think about what might have been. I can choose to let this experience turn me bitter or [let it] turn me even more to serving Christ, which is the reason for everything in missionary work. I want to choose to let this amazing Heaven-sent experience lift me and shape my future path.*

As a full-time missionary, my purpose was to invite others to come unto Jesus Christ. During my recovery I resolved to *always* fulfill that purpose, with or without a name tag.

Limited strength in my body caused me to rely more greatly on the Savior than I ever had before. In previous trials, I'd been so grateful for the Savior's Atonement to help me through hard times. Overcoming trials then felt more like a team effort between me and the Savior, with Him carrying my greater load. This time I felt I had little, if anything, to offer. The reality of being in a fallen state taught me for the first time something I had known all my life: I need a Redeemer and His Atonement.

Christ yearns for us to turn to Him and give "[our] *whole souls* as an offering unto Him" (Omni 1:26; emphasis added). The Savior wants all of us—our weaknesses, our strengths, our heartaches, our joys. As we humbly seek to turn our lives to the Lord, He empowers us and makes us into more than we could ever be otherwise. We must live for Christ no matter our circumstance or calling. As I internalized this truth, I gained an overwhelming awareness: my release was as inspired as my call, and if I had faith enough to go on my mission for Jesus Christ, I needed faith enough to be home from my mission for Him.

This is the lesson taught by Elder David A. Bednar when he asked a young married man with a life-threatening illness, *"[John,] do you have the faith* not *to be healed?"*[2] (emphasis added.)

Elder Bednar continued:

> We recognized a principle that applies to every devoted disciple: strong faith in the Savior is submissively accepting of His will and timing in our lives—even if the outcome is not what we hoped for or wanted. Certainly, John and [his wife] Heather would desire, yearn, and plead for healing with all of their might, mind, and strength. But more importantly, they would be "willing to submit to all things which the Lord seeth fit to inflict upon [them], even as a child doth submit to his father" (Mosiah 3:19). Indeed, they would be willing to "offer [their] whole souls as an offering unto him" (Omni 1:26) and humbly pray, "Father, if thou be willing, remove this cup from me: nevertheless not my will, but thine, be done" (Luke 22:42).[3]

As I sought for the strength to have faith not to be healed and not to be on my mission, I felt the Lord give me emotional and spiritual strength beyond what I could muster on my own. I gratefully acknowledged in my journal, *I have recently come to a stage in my healing that I'm so eternally grateful for. I'm still sick and at home and in the exact same circumstance, but there is a very real power through the [Savior's] Atonement and [His] grace lifting me up beyond what I can do myself. I don't completely understand it, but I can feel it. I know the strength I feel is from my Savior. I just feel so much love. He feels like my Savior and . . . my Older Brother. He feels closer and more real than [He has felt to me] in a long time, like I'm surrounded by love and by the Spirit. It feels so good.*

I began to feel once again the joy my mission plaque scripture had once brought me. It reads, "Therefore, let us glory, yea, we will glory in the Lord; yea, we will rejoice, for our joy is full; yea, we will praise our God forever. Behold, who can glory too much in the Lord? Yea, who can say too much of his great power, and of his mercy, and of his long-suffering towards the children of men? Behold, I say unto you, I cannot say the smallest part which I feel." (Alma 26:16)

The Savior's Atonement can buoy us up and gladden our heavy hearts and is our lifeline not only when we sin but also when we are obedient. The Savior

---

2 David A. Bednar, "That We Might 'Not . . . Shrink' (D&C 19:18)," CES Devotional for Young Adults, University of Texas–Arlington, March 3, 2013.

3 Ibid.

makes up for our own sicknesses, heartaches, shortcomings, weaknesses, and unfulfilled yearnings. Christ bore my burden with me. I had to learn to actively trust His help and His acceptance, remembering that the Savior lived His life to help me and others, in these very moments of trial.

The loss you feel is real, and it's okay to feel that. You had plans and dreams to continue serving your mission—good, righteous, pure desires to serve your Heavenly Father. Naturally when something changes so drastically to cause you to come home from your mission, it will hurt. Your hurt and feelings of nothingness aren't symbols of unbelief or unrighteousness. Nothing could be further from the truth. Rather, they testify of your sincerity and love for the Lord, as well as your desires to serve Him.

Remember the Savior, who died for you and who *lives* for you. Turn to Him with your pain and sorrow, your cries, and your regrets. Turn to Him with the love that carried you out on your mission. He will be there to help you. He knows the reality of everything you feel even when no one else perfectly understands. He will help you. The Atonement of Jesus Christ has a healing power that will mend your soul. Yes, you will still have the loss from missed opportunities. But ultimately even that loss, that heart-wrenching hole in your soul that leaves you so broken you don't know if there are even pieces to pick up, can and will be consumed in the Savior's all-encompassing Atonement.

When we are sorely tested and tried, when we are hurting more than we imagine we can bear, when we ache beyond what human words can even begin to express, when we feel like we have given every ounce of faith and strength we can muster, I know our Savior is with us. I can't explain it or how it is possible, but He understands. He is there to help, to calm us, to give us peace amidst our storms, to be a friend. He who allows us to be tested and tried is ultimately in control, and when we have faith in Him, He will help us. He is our rock and our salvation. We are never alone.

In time, I knew I would not be going to Korea. Although I'd received confirmations from the Spirit that I was where I was supposed to be, it didn't take away the hurt. It was difficult to explain to others that in not going to Korea I was doing Heavenly Father's will for me. It seemed especially hard for many returned missionaries who served the expected eighteen or twenty-four months to understand that two-and-a-half months really can be a full mission.

Moving forward and making new plans for my life created new challenges because I didn't know if I could trust promptings I'd received. In following the prompting to serve a mission, I'd put every ounce of faith and trust in that plan. I'd loved it and followed it and wanted it so deeply. But when it fell through, I began questioning myself and my decisions.

I had to trust that amidst so much darkness, light would come as I kept moving forward. After much prayer, I felt I was to move forward in talking to my bishop about applying for a Church Service Mission. I felt a peace greater than anything I could have imagined. It was a way I could begin serving while still recovering. I wasn't sure what would come next, but it was enough for right then, and I knew God would continue to guide my paths.

To those who feel you failed, know that the Savior loves you and is aware of you and your needs. Heavenly Father hears your prayers. You did *not* fail. Your full-time missionary service may have been cut shorter than you planned, but you did not fail. The Lord knows you and your heart, and He sees you as a returned missionary who has served fully. Do not listen to the voices that tell you otherwise—to the critics who tell you what you did wrong or how someone else might have handled your situation with more faith. Be careful not to take offense to hurtful remarks.

If anyone would have asked me at the time if I ever thought I'd be grateful to be sick and home from my mission, I don't think I would have said yes. After all, how could I be grateful that I didn't complete my mission, the Lord's errand? How could I be grateful that I never talked to a single person in Korea? How could I ever be grateful to have missed out on all of that? It would be hypocritical to profess to believe my mission call was divinely inspired and yet something from which I could joyfully walk away. It would mean I didn't value my mission and that I gave up. Yes, I could come to terms with what happened and feel at peace. But how could I ever, in good conscience, tell Heavenly Father I was grateful I came home early?

It's taken a long time for me to get to the point that I can say this and completely mean it. But I am grateful I got sick. I'm grateful I came home early. I'm grateful for my rerouted life's course.

No, I didn't want to spend all that time alone. I didn't want to come home and complete an online service mission instead of being in Korea (even though the service mission was an incredible blessing). I didn't want to have to explain to people why I didn't go to Korea. I didn't want to have my heart broken. I didn't want to be sick.

But that's exactly where the miracle is.

Heavenly Father knew better than I did what I wanted long-term. He knew I needed the experiences in the MTC. He knew the great joy I'd receive in serving the mission I served, and He wanted me to have that. But He didn't stop there. He tailored a mission just for me, in which He led me to miracle after miracle and blessing after blessing. Heavenly Father gives us opportunities and allows us to experience pain because He knows which path will eventually lead us to be happiest. That's all He wants! We are His children, and His ultimate desire is to bring us joy.

Heavenly Father hears your prayers and accepts your offering. You did make a difference, and you will continue to make a difference on whatever path the Lord leads you. He knows you perfectly and continues to guide you on a mission perfectly tailored to bless you and those around you. He will walk with you and make sure you are never alone. He loves you and loves the service you performed in His name.

Often the deepest struggle isn't remembering that Heavenly Father loves His children in general but internalizing that He loves *you*. Satan wants you to feel cast out and alone. He tries to mask every hint of Heavenly Father's love. But God's perfect love shines brighter than Satan's feeble attempts. Pray for a greater awareness of His love.

Listen to the voice of the Spirit, a member of the Godhead, who counteracts Satan's lies to remind you that you are a child of God and that Heavenly Father has even greater plans for you than you can yet see. Trust that, even though sometimes the fulfillment of God's plans and promises seems so far away.

My deepest desire as a missionary was to help other people feel loved. One particularly rough day at home after I'd been sick for several months, I prayed to God asking why. I wanted to know why I was home, why I couldn't go to Korea, why I didn't have an answer to what my body was doing, why I couldn't get better faster, and why it hurt so much. An impression came to my mind: *Kristilyn, you pray to help others. You pray for opportunities to help others feel My love. How do you expect to be able to do that without going through experiences that give you a heart?*

I believe Heavenly Father allowed me to have those lonely days and nights for months on end in order to give me a deeper awareness of His love for others as well as for myself. No, I didn't go to Korea and help people there to feel of God's love like I so desperately desired. But God answered my prayers through providing my own tailored mission that gave me a heart.

Being sick for half a year with an unknown virus gave me greater love for those who struggle for reasons unknown to me. My circumstance opened my eyes in a profound way to the realization that I have no idea what anyone around me struggles with. Everyone has trials. Everyone hurts. Sometimes the effects of that pain are visible. Frequently, the pain lies deeper. The key is that we never know. We never know how others hurt, the cause of the hurt, or what Heavenly Father's plan is in their lives. The natural man in each person often tempts us to judge too quickly and too harshly, when our first reaction should be to love and reach out. I regret the all-too-often times that I have quickly made harsh judgments about others' lives without knowing their heart.

The Savior invites us to love our brothers and sisters, to pray for understanding, to look for ways to serve them, and to be a friend. Let's be a people that pauses an extra moment before making an inconsiderate comment and instead ask our Father in Heaven how we can help those who struggle, which are all of His children. We *will* make a difference in others' lives. It is up to us whether that difference aggravates or alleviates emotional, spiritual, and physical wounds. Earthly angels are always in demand. Let us choose today to be angels to those around us, with Christ's help.

Today my heart praises Heavenly Father, saying, *"Thank you, Mr. Gardener for [having love enough] to cut me down" (see appendix),*[4] *patience enough to help me grow, kindness enough to walk with me, compassion enough to share my tears, goodness enough to send angels, understanding enough to know my heart, and knowledge enough to guide my paths.* He truly knows the details of my life. And he knows the details of yours.

4 Hugh B. Brown, "The Currant Bush," *New Era*, Jan. 1973 (used with permission).

CHAPTER 2
ALWAYS IN THE LORD'S PLANS
BY BRAEDEN SMITH (PSEUDONYM)

"But the Lord knoweth all things from the beginning; wherefore, he prepareth a way to accomplish all his works among the children of men; for behold, he hath all power unto the fulfilling of all his words." (1 Nephi 9:6)

I NEVER EXPECTED TO BE sent home early. And, in reality, I wasn't. While the ending of my mission wasn't what I anticipated it would be, I learned that the Lord has a bigger picture than I do and that my mission was exactly what He intended it to be.

Before my mission, I was eager for my call to serve. I've wanted to be a missionary for my entire life. I remember opening my call letter (it was still paper at that time) and reading that I had been assigned to labor in the Iowa Des Moines Mission. At first, I was confused; I didn't even know where Iowa was! But as I learned more about my mission, I discovered I had both Nauvoo and Carthage in my mission. I was so excited!

At the time, I thought it was interesting that my call letter said I was "expected" to serve for a period of twenty-four months. Why expected to serve? But I quickly forgot about the wording as I started to prepare for my mission.

Before leaving, I had a lot of preconceived notions about missions. I remember thinking missionaries were "perfect" people: that they were always busy teaching lessons, that they automatically qualified for major spiritual experiences, and that they saw success in everything they did. I soon found out that life as a missionary wasn't like that. It was hard on me at first, because what I had expected mission life to be, both in the MTC and in the mission field, was not what it actually was. Nothing about my current situation seemed to meet the standard I had previously set in my mind about what a mission entailed. It was a shock to me when I got into the field to discover that we weren't teaching a bunch of lessons every day. In fact, we had only a few a week. I was first assigned to serve in the Young Single Adult (YSA) branch in Iowa City, and my first transfer period serving there was between semesters at the University of Iowa, so there were very few eighteen- to thirty-year-olds around even to talk to. Many of the people we did find wouldn't keep return appointments or wouldn't keep commitments or would drop us.

Thankfully, I had a fantastic trainer who taught me a lot. The most important lesson I learned from him was how to love serving a mission. My trainer helped me see that everything we did mattered—that every part of our daily work contributed to our overall purpose as missionaries and, in some way, helped to progress the Lord's kingdom. As soon as I internalized this, I started to love each day I had as a missionary. I struggled with homesickness for only a week or two because I learned very quickly how much joy serving the Lord brought me. Although serving my mission was the hardest thing I had ever done, I gained a deep love for my life as a full-time missionary. It was incredible!

Around this time, I found a wonderful quote by Elder Jeffrey R. Holland that really hit home and had a profound impact on me. In his talk "Missionary Work and the Atonement" (Ensign, March 2001) he said,

> Anyone who does any kind of missionary work will have occasion to ask, Why is this so hard? Why doesn't it go better? Why can't our success be more rapid? Why aren't there more people joining the Church? It is the truth. We believe in angels. We trust in miracles. Why don't people just flock to the font? Why isn't the only risk in missionary work that of pneumonia from being soaking wet all day and all night in the baptismal font? . . . I offer this as my personal feeling. I am convinced that missionary work is not easy because *salvation is not a cheap experience* . . . How could we believe it would be easy for us when it was never, ever easy for [our Savior]? . . . I don't believe missionary work has ever been easy, nor that conversion is, nor that retention is, nor that continued faithfulness is. I believe it is supposed to require some effort, something from the depths of our soul.
>
> If [Christ] could come forward in the night, kneel down, fall on His face, bleed from every pore, and cry, 'Abba, Father (Papa), if this cup can pass, let it pass,' then little wonder that salvation is not a whimsical or easy thing for us. If you wonder if there isn't an easier way, you should remember you are not

> the first one to ask that. Someone a lot greater and a lot grander asked a long time ago if there wasn't an easier way. . . . When you struggle, when you are rejected, when you are spit upon and cast out and made a hiss and a byword, you are standing with the best life this world has ever known, the only pure and perfect life ever lived.[5]

This quote has stayed with me ever since. It was all right that I was having a hard time, because I wasn't the first one to have a hard time. It was all right that people wouldn't listen to me, because I wasn't the first one people didn't listen to. I knew I was not alone: Jesus Christ knew perfectly what I was feeling. This understanding helped me start to gain a more personal relationship with my Savior than I'd ever had before. I can truly say that the Savior walked the roads of Iowa with my companions and me. He was always watching over us.

Time passed, as it always does, and pretty soon I reached my eighteen-month mark. I was assigned to be an assistant to the president. The mission home had moved to Iowa City, so that meant I would be ending my mission in the same city I had started in. After six weeks there, I got a new companion, an elder who had been serving his mission for the same amount of time as me. In a little less than half a year, we were scheduled to fly home in the same group.

One day, we were in the middle of transfer planning when our mission president stopped to read an email. He was quiet for a few minutes and then said he had something to tell us that we couldn't share with anyone else yet. This happened occasionally, so I didn't think too much of it and wasn't too worried about it. But then he started explaining the situation to us. We learned that the recent spread of COVID-19 throughout the world had greatly impacted the Church's policies regarding missionaries. Many missionaries from our mission, who were at higher risk of getting the virus, would be sent home. In addition, other elders and sisters, who were approaching the end of their missions, even if they still had several months of expected service left, would also be returning home. That was the part that stung the most. My companion and I had been on our missions for twenty-one months, which meant we would be included in one of the groups heading home early. It was unreal—I never imagined I would be in this situation.

I had a really hard time wrapping my mind around the fact that my mission would be over three months sooner than I had expected. I was a little mad

5 Jeffrey R. Holland, "Missionary Work and the Atonement," Ensign, March 2001, 14–15.

at first. I felt like I had been short-changed! My companion and I had to keep this knowledge to ourselves until the next day, when we had a video conference call with all of the missionaries who would be affected by the change. That was a difficult call to be a part of. It was heartbreaking for me. Some of these missionaries would have six weeks to prepare to return home, but others were given just three days. We watched everyone's reactions to the news that they would be returning home early. Some of them were torn apart and broke down into tears, while some were visibly relieved. Both reactions broke my heart.

I never cried on my mission until the time I had to call my parents and tell them I was coming home. That was the hardest call I've ever had to make. I was crushed. My father gave me wise counsel though. He said it would be all right. He told me it was always in the plan that I would come home early. It wasn't in my own plans, he said, but it was always in the Lord's plan.

As I began transitioning my mind to the fact that I was coming home soon, I came across a scripture by Paul in the New Testament that struck me because it was written when he was in prison and about to be beheaded. Paul declared, "For I am now ready to be offered, and the time of my departure is at hand. I have fought a good fight, I have finished my course, I have kept the faith" (2 Timothy 4:6–7). This caused me to reflect on my mission, just as Paul had done with his. The scripture indicates that Paul knew beforehand that this was the end for him and that his ministry would be over, but I hadn't expected my own ministry to be over yet! All of a sudden, I was forced to realize that the time of my departure was at hand. Just days before, I hadn't known that my course—my mission—was almost through and that everything would change so abruptly. Could I say the same things Paul said? Did I finish my course, even though it was ending prematurely from what I anticipated? Did I fight a good fight, even when I hadn't expected the battle to be over already? How grateful I was to be able to reflect and say that I had truly given it my all!

When I started to come to terms with going home, I began to realize I wasn't going home for no reason. I realized I had fulfilled my mission. I had fulfilled all I was meant to fulfill as a missionary, and I had done all of the work I was meant to do in that calling. I felt so much gratitude that I had the opportunity to be an instrument in the Lord's hands to progress His work. The Spirit also reminded me how I was continuing to be an instrument in God's hands. Because of my early release and returning home at twenty-one months, an opening was created in the mission for someone else to have the opportunity to serve there. The number of missionaries allowed to serve was more strict because of the pandemic, so my early release could be the very answer to another missionary's prayer—one of someone who hadn't been out as long as I had—to be able to continue to serve. Some of my best friends were called home and then reassigned to new missions. If elders like me, who had reached twenty-one months, hadn't left to make room for them, then my friends would never have had the opportunity to be reassigned. By going home early, I was enabling other dedicated missionaries to go back out.

During my departing interview, my mission president gave me one last piece of advice. He explained that my mission was like the MTC for my life. Over the last twenty-one months, I had learned how to be a missionary. I had learned more about the gospel and gained a stronger testimony of it. I was prepared by the Lord to re-enter "normal" life, with a new mission in mind. My mission president reminded me that I am prepared now to be an instrument in the hands of the Lord for the rest of my life.

Coming home was a big change for me, as it is for everyone. I loved my mission! When I returned home, people would frequently ask me questions like what it was like or what I learned. I had a hard time answering those questions, not because I didn't learn anything but because I learned so much. I am determined to retain the lessons I learned and keep the habits I gained on my mission. I will continue daily prayer and scripture study. I will continue finding ways to serve others every day. I will continue utilizing the Atonement and becoming a new creature through Christ. I am so blessed to be able to start this new phase of life with the experience I gained from serving a mission. I know my service will have an impact on the rest of my life and on the lives of my family members, even though I didn't serve for the "expected" twenty-four months as stated in my mission call letter.

I believe that if missionaries serve honorably and come home sooner than their expected time, they are not "early-returned missionaries." They are simply returned missionaries. They didn't expect to serve for a shorter period, but the Lord had a bigger picture. It was always in His plans, even though it wasn't in theirs. Because of this, I don't think of myself as an early-returned missionary. I think of myself as a returned missionary who served with honor! How grateful I am that I had the opportunity to be called and set apart as a missionary for my Lord and Savior Jesus Christ for twenty-one months.

CHAPTER 3
NEVER ALONE
BY MARIE LEAVITT

"I will go before your face. I will be on your right hand and on your left, and my Spirit shall be in your hearts, and mine angels round about you, to bear you up." (D&C 84:88)

FOR AS LONG AS I can remember, I have wanted to serve a mission. I always loved the idea of completely dedicating a year and a half to telling people about what makes my life so wonderful. I love my Heavenly Father and thought the reason I wanted to serve a mission was because I wanted to do whatever I could to prove that love to Him. Little did I realize that maybe that would mean accepting His will for me *not* to be on a mission.

I turned nineteen in November of 2019. By then I had already submitted my missionary application and received my call to serve in the Japan Kobe Mission. I had four months to prepare to enter the MTC, during which I developed a deep love for the Japanese people and their culture. I even enjoyed studying the language. On February 19, 2020, I entered the MTC. I was nervous, but I was also so excited to get to work that it wasn't even very hard to say goodbye to my family.

The first week or so was kind of a hard adjustment, but as time went on, I started to feel the happiness and excitement about being a missionary that I had looked forward to my whole life. One night, we had just finished choir practice and were preparing for a devotional with Elder Neil L. Andersen. I remember just sitting there and feeling so happy. The Spirit was very strong. I was surrounded by hundreds of amazing people who shared my love of the gospel and my desire to serve the Lord. We were going to take His message to the entire world! It was such a wonderful feeling. Just at that moment, I had a distinct impression that I needed to start preparing for when I would go home. I needed to figure out how I was going to apply the things I had learned as a missionary to my life outside of the mission field. I had kind of a vision of myself walking off the airplane and seeing my family. While I was excited to see them, I did not want to be home and felt sad that I would no longer be a missionary. I thought this impression was really strange because I was eighteen months away from going home. It didn't really make sense for me to start preparing for that already. Still, the prompting was significant enough that I thought I should write it down.

Coronavirus existed before I went into the MTC, but I never thought it would have any direct effect on me or my mission. After I'd been in the MTC for a couple of weeks, people began to receive emails from home describing the things that were changing because of the virus. We didn't really know what to think about it because life seemed so normal where we were. After a while, we began to think we might possibly be reassigned to a mission in the United States for one transfer while things settled down. Then, as more time passed, we began to think that maybe our temporary placements might last a little longer than a transfer. One night, we were watching a devotional in our classroom when the president of the MTC announced that the MTC would be emptied by Saturday, six days later. We were all a little shocked, but it was kind of exciting at the same time. Everyone in my district started making guesses about where we would be reassigned, but the memory of the impression I received weeks before made me think I would be sent home.

Every day after that, people were being sent off to their reassignments. On Wednesday, I went to the travel office and found out I had initially been reassigned to Hawaii, but they were working on another reassignment because Hawaii had just closed its borders. Hawaii would have been perfect because I would have been able to use the Japanese I had worked so hard to learn. While I was a little sad that I couldn't go to such a cool place, I felt grateful that I was going to be able to stay out in the mission field after all. Later that day, I received an email with my travel plans to go to Las Vegas, Nevada, on Friday. Several other people in my district had also been reassigned there. I couldn't help but feel that I was just being thrown wherever there was room, but again, I was just happy that I was going to be able to serve. I felt that maybe the prompting I had received at the devotional was to prepare me to feel happy about going anywhere. That night I started packing and getting excited about what missionary life in Las Vegas might be like.

By the next morning, the MTC was already pretty empty. All three of the other sisters in my district had left, so I was without a companion. I was trying to figure out what I should do when I ran into another sister from my zone who was learning Spanish. She had already finished her designated time at the MTC and had been scheduled to leave the previous week. Everyone in her district had already left, and her teachers had even stopped coming. For some reason, all of her flight plans had fallen through. She had just been joining random classes to keep herself busy. I told her I needed a companion, and she said she had actually been wanting to join our class. It worked out perfectly!

That night, we had just sat down to eat our dinner when my name was called over the intercom. We went to the front desk, and they told me I needed to go see the MTC doctor. I immediately knew it had something to do with my asthma. I had developed very mild asthma in middle school, but it was only ever a problem when I ran long distances in really cold weather. I wasn't even going to mention it on my mission application, but my dad happened to be in the room when I was working on the medical section. He told me he thought I should mention it just to be really honest. I didn't think it would matter either way, so I did.

On our way to the clinic, I began to think about what I would say to the doctor to convince him that it really wasn't a problem. Once I was seated in front of him, he told me that studies had shown that people with asthma were more susceptible to COVID-19. I tried to persuade him that my case was different, but he just smiled politely and reaffirmed that he had been instructed to send me home. I was pretty shocked and heartbroken. As we walked out of the clinic, I told my new companion what had happened, and she immediately began to reassure me. She talked about how everything happens for a reason and how God knows what we need so much more than we do. Everything she said was inspiring and helped me to feel much better about the situation.

When my mom found out I was going to be coming home, she knew I would be devastated. She knelt down to pray that I would feel peace but felt that maybe this was going to be a good growing experience for me. She knew the other sisters in my district had already left, and her biggest fear was that I wouldn't have anyone to talk to. Instead of praying for my comfort, she prayed that I wouldn't be alone. This new companion of mine truly was an answer to her prayer!

The next morning, I got on a bus to go to the airport. I was scheduled to be traveling all day, and I was kind of dreading all the time I would have to think about how disappointed I was. Right before the bus left, an elder got on the bus and sat by me. I was able to talk to him and forget about myself. As I got on the plane, the feelings of disappointment began to resurface, but immediately the person sitting across from me turned and talked to me for the whole three hours to Texas. He had so many inspiring things to say that I couldn't help but feel that he had been sent to me from Heavenly Father.

After I got off the plane in Texas and was waiting for my final flight home to Missouri, I saw another missionary walking in my direction. As he got closer, I realized he was a missionary from my home stake. We had been good friends, but I hadn't heard from him at all since he had left on his mission to Brazil a year and a half before. He was one of the hundreds of missionaries recently sent home from that area. He had been traveling for five days and was exhausted. In the moment, it seemed like a huge coincidence that he just happened to be on the same flight as me, but looking back I realize it wasn't a coincidence at all. We talked the whole way home about the experiences we had had and our uncertainty about what was happening. It was such a blessing. Heavenly Father knew exactly how I would be feeling. While He didn't take away my sadness, He placed people in my life to help me through it.

My parents picked me up from the airport. As we drove home, I was feeling really optimistic until my dad asked if I thought maybe my service was over. He suggested I might have learned the things God had intended for me to learn as a missionary and that maybe now He would want me to move on. I immediately burst into tears. I had no idea what was going on or what the future would hold. I wanted nothing more than to go back out into the mission field, so I didn't feel like I would be able to receive any other answer about what Heavenly Father wanted me to do. I cried the whole way home.

We were told I needed to be quarantined for two weeks just in case I had picked up the virus in the airport, so I had to do mostly everything in our basement. I wanted to hug my family and talk to my friends, but I wasn't even allowed to touch anything. It did not feel like home, and I just wanted to be back in the MTC. The first few days were really hard, but I tried to have an optimistic attitude. The first morning, I woke up at six thirty and went for a run. I thought I had cleared all of my thoughts and was ready to have a good day. As I walked up to our house, my mom met me at the door, and I burst into tears again. The next couple of days were like that. I would think I was feeling better, and all of a sudden, I would just start crying. It felt ridiculous. I had always loved being home. Why was I so emotional? My family didn't understand, either, and I think it was a little offensive to them that I wasn't more excited to be with them again. At one point, one of my sisters asked me a question about the MTC. I got really excited and started rambling on about how great my experience was there. Then I realized she didn't really care about the details and was probably just trying to make conversation since I hadn't said much to anyone since I arrived. It just hurt that much more. I had had so many amazing experiences in the past five weeks that I just wanted to talk about all the time, but it seemed that nobody really cared to hear them.

In many ways, I was actually really grateful for the quarantine. It was awkward to see people who didn't know why I was home, and those who did know why didn't really know what to say. At times, I felt almost like I had done something wrong to be sent home from my mission. People tried to be really nice, but it was just more comfortable to keep to myself. As I was reading my scriptures the day I came home, I read a verse in the Book of Mormon which says,

> And now my sons, behold I have somewhat more to desire of you, which desire is, that ye may not do these things that ye may boast, but that ye may do these things to lay up for yourselves a treasure in heaven, yea, which is eternal, and which fadeth not away; yea, that ye may have that precious gift of eternal life. (Helaman 5:8)

I realized that even though I'd thought I was serving a mission because I wanted to serve God, I'd also had selfish desires. Truly committing to serve God would mean humbly submitting to whatever He might have planned for me. The things I want are going to fade away and be worth nothing in a hundred years, but going wherever God wants me is going to lead me to happiness and unimaginable treasure for eternity.

As I write this, I still do not know what is going to happen. I am realizing more and more that Heavenly Father has specific lessons He wants each of us to learn, and He knows exactly how to help us learn them. A while ago, I heard an analogy I really loved. We all seem to create a little story in our minds about ourselves and our lives. Even if we don't really like our characters in the story, we become kind of attached to them. As soon as we face something that doesn't fit with our idea of what should be happening, we think everything is falling apart. We think that in order to be good followers of Christ, we need to make Him a main character in our story when we really just need to give the whole story over to Him and let Him make of us who He wants us to be. Elder Joseph B. Wirthlin said, "David saw himself as a shepherd, but the Lord saw him as a king of Israel. Joseph of Egypt served as a slave, but the Lord saw him as a seer. Mormon wore the armor of a soldier, but the Lord saw him as a prophet."[6] We are so limited in our vision, but Christ can see who we can really become.

---

6 Joseph B. Wirthlin, "The Abundant Life," *Ensign*, May 2006, 101.

While I was in the MTC, we watched a video several times of a talk Elder D. Todd Christofferson gave. He tells a story of a farmer who found a currant bush that was very overgrown. He pruned it back and thought he saw a tear on the stump and heard the bush say, "'How could you do this to me? I was making such wonderful growth. . . . And now you have cut me down.'" In the end, the bush becomes a beautiful currant bush laden with fruit. He ends up saying, "'Thank you, Mr. Gardener, for loving me enough to cut me down.'"[7] I am confident that, one day, whether in this life or the next, I will look back on this experience and say the same thing.

I know that Heavenly Father is watching over each of us, His children. In 1 Corinthians 2:9, we read, "Eye hath not seen, nor ear heard, neither have entered into the heart of man, the things which God hath prepared for them that love him." Although I have experienced so many different emotions and feelings of uncertainty during this time, I know God can make of us so much more than we can make of ourselves. While I still don't know exactly what Heavenly Father has planned for me, I have come to recognize how He has been guiding my path all along. That knowledge has brought me much peace. Heavenly Father knows exactly what experiences we need in order to refine us into the people He knows we can become. His whole work and glory is to help us do that. As I have prayed to see God's hand in my life, it has become obvious to me that my entire life is in His hands. Through this experience, I have gained an even deeper understanding that as long as I try my best to follow Him, He will guide me to greater happiness than I can even imagine.

---

7 D. Todd Christofferson, "As Many as I Love, I Rebuke and Chasten," *Ensign*, May 2011, 98–99, quoting Hugh B. Brown, "The Currant Bush," *New Era*, Jan. 1973 (used with permission).

CHAPTER 4
HOLD ON A LITTLE LONGER
BY HEATHER CLEVENGER

"Let us cheerfully do all things that lie in our power; and then may we stand still, with the utmost assurance, to see the salvation of God, and for his arm to be revealed." (D&C 123:17)

I HAD BEEN ON MY mission in Las Vegas for a little more than four months when I was called home. Before leaving the mission field, a member gave me a stone that said Believe. I remember looking at that stone and hearing in my heart that I needed to believe in God and trust in Him and His plan. "Trust in the Lord with all thine heart; and lean not unto thine own understanding. In all thy ways acknowledge him, and he shall direct thy paths" (Prov. 3:5–6). I did not understand, but I knew God understood; this was His path for me to walk. He would not lead me astray or let me fail.

Returning home early from my mission proved to be the greatest trial of my life. This trial did not last a couple of days, weeks, or even months. It lasted up to almost two years. Even today moments of my mission and these trials still touch my heart, pulling on tender chords.

My health beforehand was fairly good. I had had struggles with back problems but had always seemed to manage it through various exercises. I knew that this one situation could possibly be the means of breaking me in the mission field, and that would soon be the case for me.

My back started to hurt beyond any pain I have ever experienced. It was so severe that pain started to shoot down my left arm, numbing my fingers. Only then I realized the position and state of health I was in. I needed medical attention. Although I went to the doctor and chiropractor on many occasions, my health was not getting better. I was at a standstill.

This time was so difficult for me. I prayed for relief from the pain and for guidance to know what to do. I talked to my mission president, my stake president at home, and my parents. All were in agreement that coming home was the best option for my health. It was an option I did not welcome or take lightly. The thought of coming home early from my mission was one of disappointment, discouragement, and failure. I had never known anyone who had come home early from a mission. Being the first in my family to serve a mission, it was a difficult will to submit to. Yet the thought and determination I had was one of getting better and returning to finish my service as a full-time missionary.

I know much more now than I knew then what the Lord had in store. It was not an easy process or a smooth ride. A mountain filled with bumps, holes, and steep hills was in my path. As I started to climb, I thought it would be the mere death of me, but God proved to me that He was there even when I thought He wasn't. He sent angels from both sides of the veil to aid me.

Prior to my mission, a plaque was given to me by my ward. It reads,

> And if thou shouldst be cast into the pit, or into the hands of murderers, and the sentence of death passed upon thee; if thou be cast into the deep; if the billowing surge conspire against thee; if fierce winds become thine enemy; if the heavens gather blackness, and all the elements combine to hedge up the way; and above all, if the very jaws of hell shall gape open the mouth wide after thee, know thou, my son, that all these things shall give thee experience, and shall be for thy good. (D&C 122:7)

I felt as though I had been cast into the pit, that wind and fire had come upon me, that the heavens had gathered blackness, and that the jaws of hell had opened its mouth to me. But as we are taught in the scriptures, "Thine adversity and thine afflictions shall be but a small moment; And then, if thou endure it well, God shall exalt thee on high" (D&C 121:7–8).

I tried to keep the perspective that what I was going through would only be but a small moment and was to be for my good, giving me experience. And if I held on and endured it, God would exalt me. Yet, not knowing what to do with my life after I returned home or the direction I was to walk, I became discouraged, and my foundation of faith began to shake. One day I sat in my room wondering, *Do I truly believe the gospel is true? I taught so many people that it was, but do I really believe it now that I am struggling with this situation?*

I could not comprehend a God who would allow such an obstacle and who would not bestow upon a worthy individual their great desire to be in the mission field serving God's children. Night after night I wondered about my testimony. *Do I believe in God? Do I believe in Jesus Christ?* Everything I thought I knew to be true seemed to be failing me in the very moments I needed them the most. Where was God when I needed Him? I had lived worthily with my whole heart ever since coming into the gospel. I knew things wouldn't be easy, but heaven wasn't answering and, from my perspective, had withdrawn altogether.

I came to a crossroads in my life at that time. I faced a decision I knew would affect the rest of my life. I could either deny my testimony and the gospel as well as the knowledge and experiences I had gained up to that point, or I could hold on a little longer. I decided to hold on.

I stopped thinking about where I was going and started taking one day at a time. Although pressing forward wasn't easy, I was supported and strengthened by a power that *did* come from heaven. I was reminded of promised blessings that awaited me, and I was encouraged by that. I was told that during my times of trial, the things that would help me carry on were those simple principles of the gospel.

I prayed most earnestly and sincerely to Heavenly Father. I was completely open with Him, telling every thought and doubt I had in my mind and heart. God knew everything I was facing before I told Him, but I have learned that this shouldn't stop any of us from going to God in prayer. As we tell Him what we are facing, we are not only allowing Him to help us through our trials, but we are helping ourselves understand more fully what we feel, think, and face.

I spent days reading the scriptures to the point that I read the Book of Mormon for seven hours each day. As I continued to read the scriptures, I opened myself to God to teach me, to help me, and to guide me.

I was consumed with determination to go back on my mission. We hear from members and Church leaders that we are to serve a full-time mission of eighteen or twenty-four months. It can sometimes feel as if those who do not serve are failures for not completing the expected period of service. I felt this strongly because I had promised God I would serve the full amount of time. Not doing so reflected, in my mind, someone who was unworthy and weak.

Frustration came as I battled to get back to my mission, with people telling me to give up and let it go, to go find someone to marry, or to go to school. Although I faced such adversity, I had the support of my parents and certain ward members who showed love, compassion, and support. They believed in me even when I didn't believe in myself.

Near the end of that year, through a difficult process and a hard realization, I came to understand that it was not Heavenly Father's will for me to return to the mission field or to be a full-time missionary again. I also learned that

God was aware of my desire and sacrifices, and He accepted them. From that moment on, I felt the Lord's approval and acceptance. However, finding my own acceptance and approval came a year and a half later.

Life was good. Things finally were beginning to settle down, and my social life was at a level of satisfaction. But one Sunday the lesson topic shook me to my core. The topic was preparing for trials. Before this time I had reflected time and time again about my mission. Being released and coming home early not to return again is a hard situation to be placed in, one that no one understands until they are actually in the situation themselves.

As the lesson was being taught, I was surprised that I was struck so deeply and profoundly. The teacher asked, "What if someone told you that the biggest trial of your life would soon come to you? How would you prepare for it? What would you do?" These questions hung on my thoughts as I reflected back. Perhaps for others in the class they were hypothetical questions, but for me they were real. For me they weren't questions for the future; they were for the past. *What did I do to prepare? If I had truly understood the trial that lay before me, what would I have done differently?*

The Lord knows what He is doing, and I came to know that He had prepared me for this trial years before I ever faced it. Appreciation came as I witnessed more and more of the Lord's hand in my life. God prepared me before my trial came, and He continuously helped me throughout (although it did not feel like it in the midst of my struggles).

For example, prayer and scripture study weren't new behaviors for me when I entered the mission field nor after my mission. Before my mission I developed the habit of reading my scriptures every day. Years before that I had developed the habit to get on my knees and pray to God every night. He soon taught me to pray not just at night but in the morning as well. It was through these simple acts that Heavenly Father prepared me and gave me strength in my life even before my mission.

Keeping the commandments of the Lord entails more than prayer and scripture study. I knew these two simple actions weren't the only things that could keep me from danger. Keeping my covenants and being obedient to the Lord's commandments gave me strength; I was blessed to see promises fulfilled by the Lord. Another thing that helped me through this time of my life one day at a time was looking forward each week to Sunday and remembering the sacrament. If I could get through one day and the next until I could partake of the sacrament, I knew I would be blessed as promised in Doctrine and Covenants 130:20–21: "There is a law, irrevocably decreed in heaven before the foundations of this world, upon which all blessings are predicated—And when we obtain any blessing from God, it is by obedience to that law upon which it is predicated." I had taught this very principle to investigators on my mission. My life now became a testing ground to apply it. As I taught it, I had believed. Now, as I lived this principle, I *knew* the truthfulness of it.

In those moments that I could not see beyond my trials to the horizon or look up to see the sun, I leaned on God, trusting in Him. As I held on, I was blessed to remember times when the Lord has shown me His love, when I felt His love. People were placed in my path to help me along, giving me encouragement and hope. Such moments helped me through these difficult circumstances during feelings of unworthiness and failure. These positive experiences sustained me, giving me hope and strength to hold on a little longer, to make it to the next day.

The Lord will prepare us for our trials, but we also need to be actively and anxiously engaged in His work. He has given us commandments to help us so that we may prepare for the storms that will rise in our lives. Preparation for trials comes by holding fast to the sure foundation of Christ, as is stated in Helaman 5:12:

> Remember, remember that it is upon the rock of our Redeemer, who is Christ, the Son of God, that ye must build your foundation; that when the devil shall send forth his mighty winds, yea, his shafts in the whirlwind, yea, when all his hail and his mighty storm shall beat upon you, it shall have no power over you to drag you down to the gulf of misery and endless wo, because of the rock upon which ye are built, which is a sure foundation, a foundation whereon if men build they cannot fall.

My continuous preparation came as I held on to the iron rod and continued down the path in obedience. It wasn't the huge earth-shattering moments of my life that sustained me but the soft, subtle, encouraging moments of the Lord's tender mercies.

As time passes, I appreciate the fact that I was sent home early, for many reasons. It has given me a drive to press forward in the service of God, understanding more fully what it means to be a member missionary or—more accurately—a lifetime missionary. The most fundamental principle I have gained is to serve *wherever* I may be. I have been blessed to find so many more ways to serve and build up the kingdom of God as I have gone through this journey. Great blessings came from this great struggle. Instead of going back on my mission, Heavenly Father blessed me to serve in other areas and, eventually, to be called as a Church Service Missionary.

I believe my faith and trust in God have grown so much more through this selected and unique path than it would have, in my individual case, if I had remained on my mission. It has fueled a fire within, and I have caught the vision of service, love, and charity. Now Heavenly Father can work with me, because I have come to trust Him more fully and more faithfully. He knows that I will do anything for Him. Just because I do not receive the desires of my heart when I want them does not mean they will not be bestowed upon me later; it just means that God has a different plan and purpose for me to fulfill now.

Although my full-time missionary service lasted only four months, I learned so much more during that service than I could ever imagine, gaining strength, courage, and leadership skills I could not have gained anywhere else. But the same is true for after my mission—I could not have gained those life-altering lessons within the mission field, nor could I have helped as many people as I did if I was still in the field.

In the moment, I could not understand why this mountain was placed before me, why the blessing of health was withheld when I had received priesthood blessings time and time again for sufficient health. Why, in the very moment I thought I needed it most, good health did not come. I was doing what I should and living the gospel worthily. I had prayed and looked to God to remove this mountain. I knew He had all power and nothing was impossible for Him.

I had yet to learn what Elder David A. Bednar has taught:

> Righteousness and faith certainly are instrumental in moving mountains—if moving mountains accomplishes God's purposes and is in accordance with His will. Righteousness and faith certainly are instrumental in healing the sick, deaf, or lame—if such healing accomplishes God's purposes and is in accordance with His will. Thus, even with strong faith, many mountains will not be moved. . . . Many of the lessons we are to learn in mortality can only be received through the things we experience and sometimes suffer. And God expects and trusts us to face temporary mortal adversity with His help so we can learn what we need to learn and ultimately become what we are to become in eternity.[8]

---

8 David A. Bednar, "That We Might 'Not . . . Shrink' (D&C 19:18)," CES Devotional for Young Adults, University of Texas–Arlington, March 3, 2013.

Instead of removing my mountain and changing my circumstances, God changed *me*. Heavenly Father knows what he wants me to be. It was through traversing this mountain that I was taught by the Lord. He humbled me and strengthened me to climb the mountain, and in so doing He gave me strength beyond my own that developed and molded me into the person He intended for me to be today.

President Dallin H. Oaks said, "Healing blessings come in many ways, each suited to our individual needs, as known to Him who loves us best. Sometimes a 'healing' cures our illness or lifts our burden. But sometimes we are 'healed' by being given strength or understanding or patience to bear the burdens placed upon us."[9]

I learned to draw closer to my Father in Heaven. No other experience would have provided me those valuable lessons. Having to come unto Christ daily, I came to know of His great love and power. Although I struggled with the idea of not returning to my mission, God helped me to see a deeper and broader perspective. I have come to see that He is in charge and that He will never leave me alone. I was taught to trust in the Lord more fully and to be patient in His plan, because the plan He has developed will be greater and sweeter than I could imagine. He changed me, He changed my heart, and He helped me draw closer to him, so that I may be a more valuable tool in His hand and an instrument in building His kingdom on earth.

As I have walked the path He has guided me down, I have become grateful for the blessings. I know that although our mountains seem great and that they may never pass, the Lord has prepared a way for us to come off conquerors. Though we may wait for the bitter cup to pass, there may be times when we need to drink it and endure our trials to the best of our ability.

Heavenly Father wants us to succeed; His desire is not for us to fail or fall. He wants us to be happy. Sometimes, in order to help us gain ultimate and eternal happiness, He must allow us to suffer, but that suffering won't be without preparation, guidance, angels, and other help from heaven.

Often it is only when we are brought low that we humble ourselves and turn fully to Heavenly Father. It is in these moments that God is able to do His greatest work and in which we are able to witness His miracles and great power. We are brought low so that Heavenly Father can bring us higher. When we hold on a little longer, He gives us strength so that through our trials, we can find His love.

---

9 Dallin H. Oaks, "He Heals the Heavy Laden," *Ensign*, Nov. 2006, 5–6.

CHAPTER 5
LOVED ENOUGH
BY BRANDT HANSEN

"For the mountains shall depart and the hills be removed, but my kindness shall not depart from thee." (3 Nephi 22:10)

My story begins not too long before I entered the MTC. I was feeling nervous and excited at the same time. There is nothing unique in this, and I think it is safe to say that almost everyone about to serve a mission has these feelings, but relying on the Lord was a huge help for me. I was ready to serve the Lord wholeheartedly for two years. I was doing all I could to be as prepared as possible to serve.

But three days before I entered the MTC, I noticed a strange lump on my wrist. I wasn't sure whether it appeared suddenly overnight, or if I just missed it slowly growing over days, weeks, months. I will never know. It didn't hurt at all, and it didn't prohibit me from doing anything that I was used to doing. When I conversed with my folks about my wrist, they had the same thoughts as I did—although we weren't really sure what it was, we weren't too worried about it and decided not to go see a doctor at that time.

I considered myself in good physical shape before my mission. I had had to keep my body core strong in order to keep my back from hurting. My back has caused me pain for as long as I can remember. But I had developed a routine to keep my core strong in order to negate the ill effects of my back. It didn't occur to me at the time that the growth on my wrist had anything to do with my back.

The day I entered the MTC, the bump was still on my wrist. I decided that if it was still there in ten days, I would see the doctor in the MTC. Why I chose ten days was not clear to me at the moment, but looking back to that decision, I now know it was an inspired timeframe.

So I put it out of my mind. I had entered the MTC! I had done it! I had officially started my mission! I had a name tag on with some Korean scribbling on it that made me super nervous but also very excited at the same time. A new chapter had started in my life. As I took my seat in our classroom where I would be attending classes for the next three months, I saw many new faces that belonged to missionaries who were just as nervous as I was. I felt overwhelmed.

Someone walked into our room and started speaking in fluent Korean to us. Not ten minutes earlier I had been with my parents at the curb, and now I was listening to an unfamiliar person uttering seemingly random sounds. I had no idea he would be our teacher. I wish I had a video of my district on our first day as our teacher got us to make our very first baby sounds in Korean: "ah," "oh," "sa," "la." What a crazy but memorable day!

By the end of that week, Wednesday through Sunday, I felt as though I had aged twenty years, both spiritually and physically. It is quite remarkable how exponential your growth is that very first week in the MTC. Looking back at my journal entries, in just four days, I could see the same amount of growth that would have formerly taken me a year to achieve.

My first Sunday in the MTC, I was called to be a district leader. I was totally dedicated to my mission, so I worked hard, along with everyone around me, to master Korean. I found it to be a hard language to learn. All through that week, I matured linguistically and spiritually. Yet my body was still the same—that bump on my wrist was still there.

The next Saturday, ten days after I entered the MTC, my companion and I went to see the MTC doctor, who in turn wanted me to go see a hand specialist because he was not quite sure what it was. The specialist diagnosed my lump as a ganglion cyst. He said it was nothing major, but I would need to have surgery to get my wrist better. Basically, my wrist fluid had something wrong with it so it had pooled into the lump on my wrist. The doctor went through the procedure with me, showing me what he would be doing in the operation.

I guess I was just shocked by the reality of it all—that I had to get surgery. I received a priesthood blessing from my zone leader for the surgery. He promised me in the blessing that I would not feel the ill effects of the surgery and that the doctor would be under control for the operation. That soothed my mind.

I went under the anesthetic by counting to ten in Korean. I woke up following the surgery a little dizzy but overall fine. It turns out that the cyst had branched out severely throughout my hand. The doctor said he was surprised when he found out I was not in pain from it because the size of my cyst should have caused much pain. I believe the Lord had blessed me not to feel the pain so that I could stay focused on my gospel and language study. Later I learned just how I much I needed that language in order to share my testimony with an investigator.

For the next couple of months, I was in a soft cast to let my hand heal properly. I couldn't move my fingers at all, so it was rather difficult to function properly. During that time, I was under doctor's orders to restrict physical activity, and I was not allowed to lift anything more than five pounds with that hand. That meant I was not allowed to do the push-ups and pull-ups I normally did to keep my back and core strong—conditioning that was essential for my well-being. So during scheduled gym time, instead of being physically active, I studied the language.

That extra language study time during gym, as well as sometimes getting up early to study it, helped a lot. It seemed I was able to stay on track with what I needed to know because of the extra effort. I was far from proficient, but I could hold a very, very simple conversation in my mission language. While my body was getting weaker, my spirituality and language were getting stronger.

I received word that the surgeon needed to give approval for me to continue on my mission. As soon as I found out *when* I would be cleared, I knew the timing was revelatory. It turned out that the healing time allotted for my hand ended just *days* before I was supposed to leave. If I had gone to the doctor before entering the MTC, I would have had to wait another transfer to enter. And if I had waited just a few more days to go see the doctor in the MTC, my hand would not have had enough time to heal before I was supposed to go. So I knew with certainty that I was to arrive in my mission field the very day I was meant to be there.

My wrist felt strange when I tried to move it after the cast was off, but I didn't care. I was headed for my mission! I knew that I had to get working the minute I set foot there. The Spirit told me that I had some big jobs to do when I first arrived, and I was eager to be the Lord's hands. My president assigned me to be with a native Korean trainer, one of only two new missionaries to get a native speaker, so it was very exciting.

That first morning, my trainer told me our dinner appointment that night was with an investigator who was not doing well. We would probably end up dropping him from our teaching pool after the appointment. So, being excited for my very first dinner appointment, I prepared thoroughly what we were going to cover that night with the brother. Again, I knew I was supposed to be in my mission area *right then;* I just didn't know for what reason. Little did I know that that dinner appointment was to be a clear example of the Lord loving *me.*

We met our investigator at a member's home, and I had a ton of fun eating with chopsticks, sitting on the ground, and immersed in the culture. After the meal we moved the tables so that we could have our lesson. My companion asked how the investigator's reading was going.

"Sorry, I didn't read," he replied.

"How is your praying going?"

"Sorry, I forgot to pray."

Suddenly, about halfway through our lesson, my companion turned to me and asked me to share my testimony. Nervously, I took a few breaths to calm myself down and then began to speak. I had never felt so good in my life than in that moment. The words just poured out in ways I had never used them before. The Spirit was very present in the room. I know without doubt I was blessed with the gift of tongues at that moment. I was not really sure what I was saying, but it just came out as if my mouth was doing its own thing. I was relying a hundred percent on what the Spirit was telling me to say, and it was just lovely. Heavenly Father really wanted our investigator to feel the Spirit. And he did.

After my testimony ended, my companion sat still for a little bit contemplating what to do next, and then very quietly he asked, "Will you be baptized by one holding the proper authority God?"

At that moment, our investigator looked at us and said yes!

Beginning from that point, this good brother changed his life with his choices. He stopped smoking and started attending church and doing all the right things. We became really close during the weeks we continued to teach him about Jesus Christ and while our investigator prepared for that great day when I watched him enter the waters of baptism.

I had done what Heavenly Father wanted me to do. I *needed* to share my testimony with our investigator in the tongue he understood. I know the Lord could have let me share what I did with our investigator with just one day of language training if He had wanted to. But He wanted to humble me and make me a better person through all the months of struggle to learn such an immensely hard language.

Not long afterward, I fell on the ice while walking. I couldn't do a full day's worth of missionary work since I needed to rest my back frequently. I was still able to go to lessons when we had them, but I couldn't do much street contacting. The pain increased. I tried all sorts of things to get my back better. I tried Western and Eastern medicine, but things were just not getting better.

I am not a crier in any form and really not that emotional overall, but I probably cried more while I was out on my mission than during any other part of my life. I remember sitting in the hospital trying to set an appointment. The soonest they could get me in was two weeks away. I sat down right in the waiting room and just cried and thought, *When is this going to be over?* I couldn't imagine waiting two weeks to begin treatments on my back. I was overwhelmed with the burden I felt at the time. I felt so alone in this foreign country, with my companion as my only support.

There was nothing comforting or *normal* in my life—everything was different. I remember those times praying at night just asking, begging for the pain to stop so I could live up to the expectations I'd set for myself.

It was during those times that the Holy Ghost reminded me of the parable of the currant bush (see Appendix). The little bush asked, in effect, *Why are you cutting me down when I was growing so well?* And the gardener admonishes (I paraphrase), *Have patience my little bush, I have cut you down so that I might raise you up into something perfect.*[12] I had grown so well in the MTC, but now I felt cut to the ground.

So during those times when the tears came and I felt all alone, I remember thinking about that talk and taking deep relaxing breaths. *I cut you down so that I might raise you up.*[13] I felt so much as I imagined the Savior had during those difficult times—with the world against me and no one to turn to. So I bucked up, wiped my tears away, and, through the power of the Atonement of Jesus Christ, drank *my* bitter cup. It was a process I had to repeat day after day, and it only worked when I focused on the Savior.

It was hard coming home, for I so loved my mission people and their culture. As I shared my experiences with the elders completing their missions who were leaving with me, they said I had experienced as much or more in my one transfer as they had experienced on their whole missions. It was an action-packed transfer.

It is difficult to say in words the emotions I had when I came home. People seemed to focus on the fact that I was home instead of on the fact that I had *served*. It was a rather difficult part to face. Not only was I battling that same focus within myself but I also had to answer all the awkward questions people posed. Sometimes it was hard not to take offense.

A few months after being home, I was on exchanges with the missionaries in my area, and we were teaching a new investigator. I was able to share my testimony with this new investigator, and she felt the Spirit. We talked about

12 See Hugh B. Brown, "The Currant Bush," *New Era*, Jan. 1973 (used with permission).
13 Ibid.

the gospel often after the missionary lessons. She confided to me that the missionaries were great, yet she also needed to have a *normal* person to share her concerns with.

When she was baptized a member of The Church of Jesus Christ of Latter-day Saints and received the gift of the Holy Ghost, I knew I had come home early in part to be able to help teach her. Although it has been hard emotionally for me to return, I feel at peace knowing my Father in Heaven has not forgotten about me and still has many wonderful things to do through me.

Now I see how things with my health were linked with Heavenly Father's greater purpose. I got the cyst on my hand. If I would have been able to exercise normally during those months, it is unlikely a fall on the ice, such as the one I had, would have done nearly the damage it did to me. But God, in his infinite wisdom, saw where and when I was needed and implemented agents to get me in those locations at the right time.

It was during those times on my mission, as I studied the gospel of Jesus Christ, that I really grew to understand the details of the Savior's Atonement, details that helped heal my soul when I came home. It was a rough journey for me. I experienced wonderful highs, such as these two baptisms, and many lows. Yet I know that through the Atonement of Jesus Christ, *all* can become perfected and made whole again. And that includes back injuries and the depression that came as a result of returning home early. My story may be far from typical of the ordinary missionary, but it is *my* story. My story is one of the life of a son of our Heavenly Father and of a brother to our Redeemer Jesus Christ. Through the tender mercies I've experienced, I cannot deny that They love *me*.

CHAPTER 6
THE WIDOW'S MITE
BY JENNIFER BALLARD

"The LORD is my rock, and my fortress, and my deliverer; my God, my strength, in whom I will trust." (Psalm 18:2)

SITTING ON THE GRASS OUTSIDE a hotel in Pocatello, Idaho, my family and I opened the call. My voice quivered as I half cheered, half cried while reading the message inside. I was called to serve in the Guatemala Guatemala City South Mission. I felt like I couldn't breathe. A flood of emotions came over me while my family congratulated me. *Guatemala!* Full of excitement and nerves, we headed over to a nearby bookstore to find a book of the country I would soon be living in. I couldn't get over the beauty of the Guatemalan culture I saw on the pages in front of me and couldn't wait to experience it. In just more than three months, I would be in the Provo MTC, and just a few short weeks after, I'd be at the Guatemala MTC.

Over the next few months, my family and I made all the preparations. We purchased my luggage, clothing, bedding, and everything else I would need. We made connections with people who had children currently serving in Guatemala and visited with them. I read anything about Guatemala that I could get my hands on. As it started to feel more real and my departure date approached, I also began to feel anxiety as I'd never felt it before. I told myself that was normal; these feelings would soon go away. I immersed myself in scripture study and frequently attended the temple. I gave my farewell talk in church, surrounded by lots of loving family members, and was set apart as a full-time missionary.

Finally the morning arrived when I would leave my family and set off on this new phase of my life as a missionary. My heart pounded all morning as I got ready. At last, I reached the top of the stairs in my grandma's house. My family wanted to have one last family prayer before leaving the house. My anxiety peaked, and suddenly I couldn't stand up. I crumpled by my suitcase into broken sobs as my family tried to coax me into the living room to pray. I didn't know it then, but this would be the beginning of many anxiety attacks.

In my life, I felt like I always did well at what I set out to do. I got good grades in school, made lots of friends, and had achieved my associate's degree with plans to complete my bachelor's after finishing my mission. I kept telling myself that the feelings of fear and anxiety would go away. The last thing I ever imagined was that in just a few short months, I would be back on a plane coming home.

I was lucky to be in the MTC at the same time as one of my brothers. Seeing him on the afternoon of my first day brought me so much comfort when I desperately needed it. I don't think he knew just how vital he was in helping me stay calm during the very beginning of my mission. I would think, *I can do this. I'm not alone.* It was so reassuring to see him every few days.

One Sunday while at the MTC, I was asked to play the piano in sacrament meeting, even though my piano skills are less than impressive. My fingers trembled as they hit the keys, and I knew chances were slim that I was actually playing the right notes at the right tempo. I felt embarrassed as I returned to my seat after the opening hymn. Soon after that, the sacramental hymn was played by an elder who was clearly a talented pianist. Later in the meeting, a counselor in our branch presidency gave a talk. He spoke about how the Lord turns our weaknesses into strengths. Looking right at me in the congregation, he told me that he was moved upon by the Spirit when I played the piano because he knew that it had taken every fiber of my being to play that song. He knew it had taken all the courage I could muster and all the connections between my brain and fingers needed to play that hymn. I started to cry silently. My music had brought the Spirit? The Lord spoke to me through this leader, telling me that my very best effort was exactly what the Lord needed, and He was grateful for all of my energy and faith. My humble offering had been received with gratitude from on High. Heavenly Father knew me and loved me and was thankful for my sacrifice, even though it was only a small offering compared to what another could give.

Although my feelings of anxiety continued to increase, I had an incredible support system. The district I was placed in was perfect for me. I felt like I belonged with them, and there were times I was able to help support other missionaries around me from my district. We worked hard in class to study the gospel and learn Spanish. We enjoyed singing the hymns from the children's songbook in Spanish as we'd get ready for bed, and I felt like we genuinely enjoyed being together.

After three weeks of living the MTC life, my companion and roommates walked me to the bus early one morning to depart to Guatemala. Again, my nerves began to increase and I told myself it was a phase—completely normal. *There's nothing to worry about.* I met up with missionaries at the airport who would be in my new district. We flew to Texas. Boarding the plane in Texas was completely horrifying to me, which didn't make any sense. I had lived away from home for three years at this point. I'd flown on planes before and loved trying new things. It just didn't make any sense to me why suddenly, now that I was boarding the flight to Guatemala, I felt completely sick to my stomach. I did not want to board that plane. I gathered all the courage I could muster and stepped inside.

The next six weeks were similar to the experiences I'd had in Provo. Due to the tiny missionary population in the Guatemala MTC, everyone knew each other. This created what I felt was a very safe environment for me to progress in my mission and feel comfortable. My anxiety leveled off, and I was able to make new friends, continue to study the gospel, and practice my Spanish even more. There were parts of being in the Guatemala MTC that I absolutely loved. I loved their theme, [Leave things] *better because you were there!* My companions were wonderful, and actually being in Guatemala was exciting. We were able to attend a weekly session at the Guatemala City Temple, which was right across the street. I loved the little pieces of their culture I could see as we had little field trips through the city. I instantly loved every Guatemalan I spoke with and was thrilled to be serving my mission in such a beautiful city with the sweetest people, yet the further along I got in my mission, the more frequently I experienced severe anxiety attacks. When they came, I would pray harder than ever before. The pain would subside for a little while, but every time the anxiety would come back stronger than before. By the time I left the Guatemala MTC, I had convinced myself that everything would be okay, and I was eager to get started.

My enthusiasm was short-lived, however, and the fire that burned within me quickly burned out. Once I was in the field, it didn't matter how much I loved the sweet people we met and shared lessons with, how fervently I prayed or studied my scriptures, or how often I would try to push the worry aside. I realized very quickly that my heart was broken. It wasn't just a *fake it till you make it* or *toughen up* matter. I was no longer myself. I thought constantly of the scripture engraved on my missionary plaque back home in Idaho: "Therefore, fear not, little flock; do good; let earth and hell combine against you, for if ye are built upon my rock, they cannot prevail. . . . Look unto me in every thought;

doubt not, fear not." (D&C 6:34, 36) I wanted more than anything to forget myself and get lost in the work of God. Over and over for the months of my service, I had been praying for that very thing, all the while trying to trust in Heavenly Father and fear not. I wanted so much to leave things better because I was there. Yet somehow, my heart continued to break and I couldn't pull myself out of the depression I had sunken into. I was devastated.

When the depression caused me to return home after serving for only three months, I couldn't even look at myself in the mirror. I felt worthless, convinced that no one could ever love me. The life I had envisioned seemed so far out of reach. Worst of all, I had let down God and, contrary to the Guatemala MTC theme, I felt that nothing was better because I was on my mission.

As much as I wanted to go back to serve the remaining months of my mission, I knew there was no way I could, because my anxiety had increased to the point that I was in a constant state of panic.

I have been blessed with the most incredible family. They were there at the airport, embracing me when I felt I didn't even deserve it. My dad took work off the next day to be with me, and my mom tried so hard to help me cope, through lots of long talks.

It was so hard to pray when I first came home. I didn't feel worthy of God's love. I've always been told that the times you don't want to pray are when you need to pray the most. So I pushed through the pain, even though sometimes all I did was cry. Heavenly Father answered those prayers. He knows exactly what we are saying, even when the words won't come.

Upon my return home, my mom came into my room to tell me that my mission was like that of Abraham and Isaac. God commanded Abraham to sacrifice his only son, Isaac, the son for whom he had waited his whole life. I'm sure it broke Abraham's heart to walk with Isaac up the side of that mountain with the intention of binding him and laying him on the altar. I can't come close to imagining this father's heartache as he prayed to God and started to bring the sharp tool down over his cherished son. Just in the moment when he would have completely followed through with the sacrifice, God stopped him and provided a lamb in Isaac's place (see Genesis 22). My mom believed my mission was just like that. I had followed through, I had worked and served and prayed with all the energy of my heart, time and time again until, at last, the Lord delivered me. He asked me to complete a full-time mission, and for me, that mission was three months.

Before coming home, the missionary psychologist I spoke with told me I would quickly feel like myself again, but that wasn't the case. I spent the next three years wondering if I should serve another mission, even though every time I considered it, I couldn't bear the thought. I had to move on and find ways I could serve from home. I went back to BYU-Idaho and did the best I could to serve faithfully in my callings there. I volunteered in the baptistry at the Rexburg Temple. After a couple of years, I graduated with my bachelor's degree in elementary education. I've now taught first and second grade for four years, and although I'm not able to share my testimony with my students or talk about church, I help them feel God's love through me. I am now married to the most amazing and supportive husband, and I feel incredibly blessed in my life.

Heavenly Father works in mysterious ways. I don't at all regret going on a mission. I'm grateful I went and had the experiences I did. Because of what I went through, I am able to relate to people I otherwise would not have been able to, including my own brother. Only one year after I came home, he also came home early. He fell into his own deep depression. It crushed me to watch someone else go through feelings similar to those I had been through, feelings I would never wish on anyone. My brother would look at his patriarchal blessing and have no idea anymore how he could ever be the person it spoke of. I remember us sitting on our couch in the basement, crying. I testified to him that no matter what we had to go through, no matter how distanced we felt from God, there is always a way back to Him. With open arms, our Father pleads with us to come to Him.

To those of you who are weighed down with the heavy emotions that accompany returning home early, cling to the truth that Heavenly Father loves you! More than ever, surround yourself with people who love, support, and build you in order to become your best self. These are people who see the real you, the person God sees when He looks at you. I believe Heavenly Father handpicked certain family members, friends, and ward members to help me regain my self-worth when I needed it the most. Find the word of God that speaks to you. The bulk of my scripture reading at the time was in Psalms and Proverbs. The words uplifted me and gave me strength for each day. Pray more than you ever have before, even if the words don't come out. It's hard to see what Heavenly Father sees in us with our cloudy natural-man vision. Don't allow the devil's lies to trick your mind into thinking you are broken beyond repair. It isn't true. Our Creator, our Heavenly Father, loves us. We are His.

Although I didn't move mountains, convert people by the dozens, or even stay for the anticipated time of service, I did the best I could at that time. Mark 12:41–44 states, "And Jesus sat over against the treasury, and beheld how the people cast money into the treasury: and many that were rich cast in much. And there came a certain poor widow, and she threw in two mites, which make a farthing. And he called unto him his disciples, and saith unto them, Verily I say unto you, That this poor widow hath cast more in, than all they which have cast into the treasury: For all they did cast in of their abundance; but she of her want did cast in all that she had, even all her living."

Just as this widow gave her two mites to the Lord, missionaries who served with every fiber of their being are blessed for giving all they have, even if they return home early. Heavenly Father is *still* grateful for the widow's mite of a mission I offered.

The offering of my mission is so similar to the offering of my song on the piano that Sunday in the Provo MTC. As a missionary, I gave all that I had, every single piece of my heart, to God, even with the imperfections. I am eternally grateful for the missionary experiences I had. It was far from what I anticipated, but it was exactly what I needed. There were individuals I met on my mission who have impacted my life forever. Although I battled anxiety and depression on my mission, I saw miracles every day and am forever changed from that mission where I learned to love complete strangers, a new culture, and myself. I love my Father in Heaven so much more for allowing me to serve the mission that refined me into the person I am today.

CHAPTER 7
A FULL OFFERING
BY BRITAIN BASHORE

"This will I do that ye may stand as witnesses for me hereafter, and that ye may know of a surety that I, the Lord God, do visit my people in their afflictions."
(Mosiah 24:14)

One Monday evening, my companion and I had just finished sharing a message with one of our favorite families. It was a very spiritual lesson, and we felt that they were well prepared for what we had to share.

Earlier that day, we had received numerous text messages from our mission president, as well as an email, telling us to prepare for a quarantine because of COVID-19. Many of the text messages directed us to purchase food and supplies that could sustain us for a month of living in our apartments. We received extra funds from the Church to help us make these purchases. My companion and I bought lots of rice, canned food, and pancake mix to prepare for our quarantine. While walking home, we talked about the text messages received earlier, and we both felt that the lesson we'd just taught could quite possibly be one of the last ones we would teach in person for a while.

The next morning, while my companion and I were eating breakfast, we received another text message from our mission president. It said that the president of the Philippines, Rodrigo Duterte, had given foreigners one week to return to their home countries before the borders of the country would be closed to prevent the spread of the virus. Our mission president told us to pack our belongings quickly and head to the mission office. We were in shock as we quickly packed some of our important things. I couldn't believe it. Everything was changing so fast. I couldn't stop myself from wondering what was next in God's plan for me. We were hustling, so we left our sheets on our beds and a few shirts and pairs of pants hanging in our closets. We took all of our rice and pancake mix and put them in the refrigerator to be protected from rats and insects. We figured that because only the foreigners were leaving, maybe some of the Filipino missionaries who were able to stay in the mission could make use of the clothes and all of the food we had purchased.

We met up with another American on our way to the mission office, and he told us about how he had left his Filipino companion with a member of the bishopric in his area. He said his companion was sad to see him go and had quite a few feelings of uncertainty. Looking back on this experience, I feel grateful that I had an American companion traveling with me and sharing some of the same stresses so I didn't have to go through this transition alone.

At the mission office in Bacolod City, we had a short meeting in which my mission president expressed his love for all of the departing foreign missionaries. After the meeting, we loaded onto buses headed to a small town called San Carlos City, located on the other side of the island, where we would pick up a few missionaries from a neighboring mission. From there, we were going to board a barge from San Carlos to get to Cebu City on a neighboring island. The plan was to travel in a large group together. Little did we know it would be days before we could actually fly home.

Upon our arrival in San Carlos City, missionaries from the Cebu East Mission boarded our buses, and we waited together for a few hours. We were told to social distance by sitting in every other seat on the bus. We sang hymns together as we waited for our buses to be loaded onto the barges. However, after a few hours of waiting, we were informed that none of the barges would be permitted to travel to Cebu City, so instead, we slept in a nearby hotel. Then, in the morning, we headed back toward Bacolod.

As we drove, we were stopped at a checkpoint a few miles away from Bacolod City. To prevent the spread of the virus, officials were trying to slow down traffic from other parts of the country entering major cities. We weren't allowed to pass through the checkpoint because we had picked up missionaries from the other side of the island. To avoid any attention from the media, the buses traveled back a few miles away from the checkpoint and parked on a narrow road in the middle of a large sugarcane field. Everyone in our group prayed and read scriptures while we waited for permission to cross the checkpoint. We closed all of the blinds on the windows, and then we spent the remainder of the night on the bus waiting for any travel updates and trying to sleep.

The next morning, we received excellent news: our mission president had contacted some of the leaders of Bacolod, and we got permission to cross the checkpoint and at last enter into the city.

After crossing the checkpoint, we headed to a chapel in a small town near Bacolod, where we had another meeting with our mission president and a few local leaders. We were told that the Church had chartered five airplanes to take all of the American missionaries home. The chartered airplanes were all in Manila, and another airplane was scheduled to take us to Manila from Bacolod the following day. We spent the night in the nearest church. Before going to sleep, many of us took showers in small makeshift showers that local Church leaders had made in the bathrooms, using a bucket of water and a smaller bucket. Later that night, we were each given a shiny metallic sheet of insulation that looked similar to an emergency blanket, and we all slept on the floor in the chapel.

The following morning, we traveled to the Bacolod-Silay Airport, where we boarded a small airplane and flew to Manila. Upon arriving, I felt shocked to see such a large airport full of missionaries from surrounding missions. We then boarded buses and headed to a large hotel nearby and spent another night in Manila before leaving for the United States the next day. General Authorities and local Church leaders arrived in the morning to help us load onto buses headed from the hotel to the airport. Again, we received instructions to sit in every other seat to follow social-distancing guidelines.

Before my bus left the hotel, Elder Taniela B. Wakolo of the Seventy climbed aboard and told us that he and Heavenly Father loved us and were grateful for our help in gathering scattered Israel.

Once we reached the Manila Airport, we were all handed our boarding passes. My companion and I had stuck together all the way up to this point, when we found out that we had been assigned to sit in different sections of the plane: my seat was in first class, and he was flying in economy.

After taking my seat, I looked back and joked with the missionary behind me, "Wow! What do you think we did to deserve this?"

He responded cheerfully, "We are just being blessed for our obedience, Elder!" It was nice to see that all of the missionaries were in a good mood, even the ones who weren't in first class!

After takeoff and a few hours in the air, we landed in Tokyo, Japan, for a short refueling. After about an hour, we took off again and, after many more hours in the air, landed in Salt Lake City the next day. I remember looking out the window before landing and seeing some of the familiar mountains surrounding the valley. All of the mountains were capped in snow. I never thought I would be coming home to such a sight. I had left in August and thought I would be coming home in August to nice warm weather, not a brisk day in March. After landing, I quickly remembered how cold it can be in Utah. We waited for our luggage just outside of the airport, but after searching for a while, quite a few of the other missionaries and I couldn't find our belongings. We soon learned that many of the bags had gotten mixed up during the different flights. Tired of waiting for my lost luggage and deciding to worry about it later, I looked over at the parking garage and found some familiar faces looking at me and shouting, "Welcome home!" I rushed up the stairs of the parking garage to my family. They quickly pulled me away, and we all got in the car and headed for home.

Throughout all of this, I had had the understanding that I was going to live with my family for a few weeks and then get reassigned somewhere in the United States to continue my missionary service. Before I arrived, though, my family found out that all of the missionaries who had longer than six months remaining on their missions would be reassigned. Missionaries who had less than six months left on their missions, however, would be honorably released from their missionary service. On the ride home, my dad explained that I was finished with my mission because I had a little over five-and-a-half months left and fell into the latter group, who would be honorably released.

It was hard for me to believe. My mission was finished. I felt such a jolt as the reality set in that my mission had been cut short from what I had anticipated. While driving home, my dad also told me that our stake president would come over later that day and formally release me from my calling. It felt strange to finish so abruptly something that I had been so completely involved in. I'd felt like I had a great purpose in the Philippines, and now I wasn't sure what I was going to do with all the extra time I had at home before heading to school in the fall.

It was strange seeing things on the way home that I recognized from before my mission. It was also strange to see some things that had changed. I remember walking back into my house and feeling dizzy. The culture shock was really getting to my head. I thought it was crazy that I could drink out of the sink without getting any parasites. And, after having taken cold-bucket showers for nineteen months, I remember thinking how blessed I was to live in a house with warm water. Where are the mosquitos? and Where are all of the ants and lizards on the walls? were questions that kept coming to mind. I could not believe how clean my house was!

When dinner was ready, I remember feeling strange eating with my fork in my right hand and not seeing any rice on the table. Everything was different at my home in America from my home in the Philippines. Every once in a while, I would say a word in Hiligaynon and wonder why my family couldn't understand me.

After my stake president released me, he asked me if I had enjoyed the mission, and instead of giving a good, thoughtful answer, all I could say was, "Yep. It was good." I was still in shock. The initial shock lasted for several days, and I continued to struggle with the transition for weeks after being released. I remember waking up early for quite a few days and going through my regular missionary schedule and reading my scriptures for hours. I felt like I was sinning when I watched TV or movies with my family. I didn't even want to listen to music in the car unless it was from the Tabernacle Choir at Temple Square. It was also difficult for me just to find my place in my family. I felt like I didn't really belong. I felt weird not having a companion all the time, and being alone was uncomfortable.

When I was in the Provo MTC, one of my teachers told our class about how much going to the temple had helped her adjust to being home after her mission. In my mission, we didn't have a temple, and the only opportunities I had to go to the temple as a missionary had been while I was in the MTC. While in the Philippines, I had set goals to go to the temple each week when I got back to Utah after my mission. Sadly, completing this goal was not an option when I returned because all of the temples were closed due to the pandemic. I needed a different plan to help me adjust to life as a returned missionary.

One day, I had planned on reading some of my emails on my missionary portal. Upon opening the portal, I saw a video put out by the Church. In the video, Elder Dieter F. Uchtdorf of the Quorum of the Twelve Apostles spoke about the difficult times created in missionary work by the coronavirus. He spoke about missionaries who were still in the mission field, missionaries who were reassigned to new locations, and missionaries, like me, who were honorably released from their missions. I remember feeling comforted as he said,

> God is at the helm. He loves you and knows your individual circumstances, thoughts, and challenges. I want you to know that He always provides a way for us to find happiness and joy even in the midst of challenges. He said on the night before He died, 'These things I have spoken unto you, that in me ye might have peace. In the world ye shall have tribulation: but be of good cheer; I have overcome the world' (John 16:33). The First Presidency and Quorum of the Twelve Apostles love you. Your well-being and safety are of great concern to us.[14]

---

14 Dieter F. Uchtdorf, "A Message of Encouragement to All Missionaries and Families," video message to missionaries of The Church of Jesus Christ of Latter-day Saints, March 24, 2020, 2:41.

I was grateful to hear Elder Uchtdorf express his love and concern for all of the missionaries. I loved listening to an Apostle share his testimony of God's love for His children.

Later, Elder Uchtdorf spoke directly to missionaries who were sent home because of the pandemic. He said,

> Some of you have been released as missionaries earlier than you were planning. You may feel that your missions have been cut short. However, please rest assured that you have served faithfully. You accepted the call! Know that your mission was a full offering. You have done everything you were expected to do. Thank you for your dedicated service! Remember, you will always be a missionary! You will always be following the Savior's invitation to minister to all, inviting people to come and see, come and help, and come and stay.[15]

His testimony that what I had done was a full offering brought me comfort. Before I heard him say this, I had been contemplating how I was going to make up for the remaining five-and-a-half months of my mission. I felt like I needed to do something miraculous, but I felt peace hearing that I had done what was expected of me. It also meant a lot to me to hear that I will always be a missionary and that I can always help others come closer to the Savior, even if I am no longer serving a full-time proselyting mission.

Adjusting back into my life at home has been a challenge, but I know the Lord will provide a way. I have been able to find peace and happiness through studying the Book of Mormon each day and spending time with my family. I also regularly talk to the friends I made in the Philippines, and I love hearing about ways they continue to strengthen their faith and endure to the end. Knowing they love the Lord and continue to strive to be more like the Savior brings me joy.

I have seen so many blessings come from my missionary service. I know the Lord is hastening His work in His vineyard and that His work will continue on through the millennia. Coming home from a mission is hard, but I know Heavenly Father is grateful for all of the missionaries, no matter the length of time or location of service, and for the work that they have done while in His vineyard. I know God wants His children to be happy and that our trials help us become what He needs us to be.

---

15 Dieter F. Uchtdorf, "A Message of Encouragement to All Missionaries and Families," video message to missionaries of The Church of Jesus Christ of Latter-day Saints, March 24, 2020, 5:08.

CHAPTER 8
AN INSTRUMENT IN HIS HANDS
BY CHRISTOPHER HOVIS

"Therefore, let your hearts be comforted . . . for all flesh is in mine hands; be still and know that I am God." (D&C 101:16)

My mission was years in the making. The first time I can remember wanting to be a missionary was when my family was being taught the gospel in Virginia. My dad was a convert to the Church when he was in his teens and then fell away when he got relocated in the Navy. He simply lost complete contact with the Church. It was almost a miracle that the missionaries stumbled upon us.

The elders who found us were going to an appointment they had with an investigator in the neighborhood. They knocked on our door to see if they could park their car in front of our house. My dad, who had answered the door, said to them, "Sure, as long as you come teach my family after your appointment." I can hardly imagine what went through those elders' minds that day! They came back an hour later and began what I now consider one of the most important times in my life. My family and I converted to the gospel that year, and I soon came to realize that we were pioneers for our extended family.

Going through the Young Men program at church was also a good experience because my leaders didn't just tell us to go on missions, but instead they tried to show us by example why a mission was important. They taught me that a mission would prepare me for the rest of my life.

By the time I was eighteen and going into my senior year of high school, my heart was set on leaving for the mission that summer. I went through the typical amount of mission preparation that most young men go through, including early morning seminary. The one thing that changed inside me during that year was my true desire to serve the Lord. I began praying fervently and with real intent to go to a place where I could really be an instrument in the Lord's hands. I began fasting with a purpose, which for me was huge; before this time, I had always fasted with no real purpose.

I also noticed that the more I read the scriptures and studied the missionary lessons, the more questions friends asked me about the Church. Just about the time I was submitting my mission papers, I learned that as long as you're prepared to serve, then the Lord will use you as an instrument no matter where you are living. This lesson was just settling into my testimony as I received my mission call to Panama. I just never knew how that lesson would play out over the next few months.

My nerves were pretty high because no one in my family had ever served a mission for the Church and I didn't want to let my family or myself down. Little did I know then that my time at the missionary training center in Provo, Utah, and the diagnosis I was about to be given would change my outlook on my mission and my life.

Going to the MTC was an amazing experience for me because I had never been to Utah or seen the Rocky Mountains. To be right next to those huge creations was truly something to behold. Being introduced to my district was great as well. We were to be together for the next seven weeks. Some of us were heading to Panama, some to Spain, and the rest to various missions throughout Central America.

I learned within my first week that we were all there with our own personal sorrows as well. During those seven weeks, one member of my district was sent home, another discovered a baseball-sized tumor on his foot, my own MTC companion needed knee surgery from an injury he sustained, and another elder's best friend died in a car accident. These trials weighed heavily on all of us, because the MTC truly taught us how to be like a family with our districts and companions. We developed Christlike love and charity for each other.

About halfway through those seven weeks, I attended a talk by a member of the Seventy who spoke on the real war being waged in the world. He explained that the two sides are the Lord's and the adversary's. Both sides have their soldiers and their implements of war. On the adversary's side, we see society destroying gospel principles such as the importance of marriage and the family. On the Savior's side, there are faithful members of the Church who are willing to live by faith. We, as members of the Church, need to prepare ourselves every day by doing the small and simple things such as true prayer and scripture study. We need this because we are living at the front lines of this war. This member of the Seventy taught me that this war is not just for the missionaries to fight, but instead it is for all of us to stand up for truth wherever we are. We don't have to wear a black badge in order to serve and represent the Lord and His gospel.

I felt that the Lord placed me in my district to be a support for those who needed it during those major trials. I didn't realize He had other plans in mind for me. During my seventh week, I started having severe shakes in my hands. I tried to conceal it from everyone because I thought it was from nerves from not learning the language very quickly. But one night at dinner, I was almost in tears because I couldn't eat the peas on my plate. This sounds silly, but my hand tremors had gotten so bad that I couldn't keep peas on my spoon, and my companion noticed. The next day he convinced me to go see the doctor to make sure everything was fine. Looking back, this was the right decision to make, even though I feared it might mean a chance of not going to Panama with the rest of my district the following week.

The doctor at the MTC was stumped and couldn't figure out why these tremors were occurring. He ran a number of tests and none of them showed anything wrong with me. He then sent me to a neurologist, and still nothing came up. I started feeling good that they couldn't find a reason for my shakes and thought maybe they would soon just say it was my nerves.

The final test the doctor ran was a thyroid blood test. This test simply looks at how much thyroid hormone is in your body. The thyroid is a vital organ in the body because it controls your metabolism and energy levels. If you have too little hormone—hypothyroidism—you have no energy and you can become depressed. If you have too much hormone—hyperthyroidism—you can have a number of symptoms, such as rapid weight loss, rapid heartbeat, and nervousness. My diagnosis came in, and my test showed that I had a serious case of hyperthyroidism. The MTC doctor believed that, if left untreated, it could have developed into what is called a thyroid storm. This can be a life-threatening situation if not fixed immediately. Those are the only words a doctor needs to say for the MTC to send you home within twenty-four hours.

It broke my heart to be in my room packing to go home. The feeling of pain was one of the worst that I had ever felt. I was lost because what I had been planning to do for the next two years was gone within minutes. I also felt guilty because I had the mantle of being the first missionary from my whole family to serve. It was like being a pioneer who was told to turn around and not head for the Salt Lake Valley. I had seen many missionaries with many different difficulties in the MTC, and most of them were able to continue on with their missions, while I was being sent home for an uncertain amount of time. All I was told was that I was going to be released, and that was that.

I had so many feelings going through my mind, and none of them were joyous. I began to pray, pleading with the Lord to help me through the next period of my life. I asked to know why I had even been sent to the MTC in the first place. That prayer led me to one of the most spiritual miracles in my life.

My final night in the MTC consisted of a devotional and then a testimony meeting in our classroom with our district. I could not ponder on the message of the devotional because of the weight on my mind. After the devotional, my companion and I had to take the elevator to our classroom because his knee was still healing from his surgery. Missionaries were rarely allowed to take the elevators. While standing in the elevator, my reason for being in the MTC at that time became apparent.

An older woman who was standing next to me couldn't stop looking at my nametag. I asked her if she knew me, and she said, "No, but I know your name." When we got off the elevator, she was about to cry, and she began to tell me her story. She had worked diligently in family history, and one of her distant family lines was the same as my surname, my direct line. She said that a year prior to our meeting in the MTC, she had been doing work on the line when she suddenly couldn't find any more information on that family. This made her really sad, so she began to pray and fast for the Lord's help. She prayed daily for this and fasted monthly for a year.

She said she was about to give up when she looked over and saw my nametag. She told me I was an answer to her prayers and fasting and that through me she would be able continue the work. She was right. I was able to give her my parents' contact information, and she then was able to connect with our family's genealogical data, which helped her continue her work. She also told me it was even more of a miracle because she and her husband were supposed to have been released from their MTC calling a week prior to our meeting yet had been asked to stay for one more week.

This whole experience showed me how connected we all truly are. Miracles do happen, and the Lord uses us as instruments in His hands to answer prayers and bless others. I didn't know why no one ever discovered my hyperactive thyroid before, but what I do know is that the Lord needed me to be at the MTC at the exact moment I was there. This experience was an answer to both my prayers and the woman's and gave me the strength and courage to go home the next day with faith that the Lord knows what is best for us.

While home was not where I wanted to be, it was where I needed to be. When I left the MTC, the doctor told me I would most likely be home for more than four months, so they decided to release me.

The first Sunday home was very strange. I had returned on a Friday, so by Sunday no one had heard I was coming home. When I walked into the church building, no one came up to me to say hi or ask me how I was doing. In fact I got the exact opposite. Members I had known for years avoided me as if they didn't even know me. Other than having my parents there, I felt completely alone.

Just as I sat down in the chapel, my bishop came up to me and greeted me very warmly. He asked if I wanted him to say why I was home, and I very eagerly said, "Yes, say as much as you want." So he did exactly what I asked. He explained that I was home for medical reasons and that I should be able to return to the mission within the year. When sacrament meeting ended, just about the whole ward came up to me, hugged me, and greeted me. I felt really strange, because an hour earlier it seemed like they'd all assumed I had done something horrible. Either way it taught me to treat everyone the same whether they come home for medical or non-medical reasons. Judgment of others only creates emptiness in the victim and leaves no one happy. We should always strive to build each other up with love. If someone is in church, it means they are striving to become better than they are.

The MTC doctor had counseled me to find an endocrinologist, who would be able to treat my condition effectively and help me through my recovery. He then told me I most likely would not be able to be seen by one of these specialists for at least six months because there are not many of them and all of them have many patients. That first Sunday home, I sat down with my bishop in his office after church. As I told him about my condition and what needed to happen to get me back into the mission field, he began to smile. He then told me I was in luck because he worked as a doctor at the university hospital where he would be having a meeting with one of the area's only endocrinologists the following day. A sense of peace such as I had never felt before came into my life.

Suddenly the issue of finding a doctor was gone because my bishop would be able to work me into his colleague's schedule. Sure enough, the next day I received a phone call from the office of the endocrinologist and was told that they could see me that very week. This truly was a miracle. I asked the nurse on the phone what the normal waiting time for this doctor was, and she told me six to eight months. The Lord places people in our lives for a reason.

There were more nerves building up inside of me going home than there had been going to the MTC. The main reason was because I had no real path or outline in my head of what to do next. Even though I was able to get a great doctor very quickly, there was still the issue of trying to get back into the mission field within four months, which then was the normal timeframe the Church allowed before you were called to a new mission. I decided that very first week home that if the Lord wanted me to go to Panama, then He would get me there. If not, He would send me somewhere else. Either way, I placed it all in the Lord's hands and did all I could do to get better.

Going through treatments for my medical issue was not fun. I had two options: either go through surgery to remove the thyroid gland or be part of a new study in which they would use radioactive iodine to kill the thyroid without physically removing it. I decided to take the second option and let the iodine kill the thyroid over a seven-week period. Even though I knew the surgery would be quicker, I just felt that taking the radioactive iodine would be in my best interest. All I had to do was drink the iodine and then wait for seven weeks. The procedure was performed two months after I arrived home, so time was ticking. I hoped the treatment would work.

The first couple of weeks of doing the treatment weren't bad, and I felt normal. I was blessed during this time with the association of other members of the ward to whom I was very close. Many members of the ward took me to the temple with Spanish members so I could listen to some Spanish and keep up my learning. I also got to teach a Spanish class at the ward building, which was a challenge and a great opportunity for me to keep my focus on the goal of going back into the mission field. I also had the opportunity on a weekly basis to work with the local missionaries, practicing the lessons and bearing my testimony to their investigators. Keeping me involved in the work helped me keep my heart set on serving more and more.

By week five I was in bed most days because by then my thyroid had been killed, and I was feeling the effects of having no thyroid hormone in my body. This was one of the most miserable times in my life. I gained weight very quickly, had no energy, and was stuck in bed most of the day. By mid-December I was given a thyroid hormone pill to balance out my levels and get me back to a normal level. I was told to take this pill for the rest of my life. During the first year I would need my blood drawn every couple of months to make sure the pill was giving me the correct dosage.

I had to depend upon the Lord during this time. The desires of my heart were to return to the mission field, but for my nearly four months home I didn't hear a word from the Church at all, either about *when* I would be returning or even *if* I would be returning. I began to pray fervently for the Lord to guide me where to go or whom to talk to. I didn't have a contact number, and I just didn't know what to do.

My prayer was answered a week later. A couple of days after Christmas, I was sitting at home when the phone rang. When I picked up, a voice on the other end said, "Elder, I am president of the Panama mission. I would like you to be one of my missionaries, and I only have three days to get you here before you are called somewhere new. Will you be at the airport tomorrow?" My heart leaped for joy, even though I was still very exhausted from trying to get my hormone levels normal. I couldn't help but begin to cry. I told my mission president I would of course be at the airport bright and early the next day.

The Lord prepares us for the experiences in our lives. He truly answers our prayers no matter what our circumstances are, and He is just waiting to bless us. We simply need to ponder what we desire and seek to know our Heavenly Father's will for us. Going back to the mission wasn't easy at all. But as I put full faith and trust in the Lord, He guided me to experiences that will stay in my mind forever. We will be tested in this life when we least expect it—we just need to decide how we will move forward and do so with faith. It doesn't mean we can't be a little scared, but we will find comfort through the gospel as we do what is right.

CHAPTER 9
OPEN DOORS
BY RACHAEL MILLER

"Eye hath not seen, nor ear heard, neither have entered into the heart of man, the things which God hath prepared for them that love him." (1 Corinthians 2:9)

I planned my whole life around my mission. Sure, like most other girls, I told myself that if I found *the one,* I would marry him instead, but I planned to go on a mission. I took three or four different mission preparation classes from institute, the stake, and my wards. The actual mission application process started a little rough. My bishop was new at dealing with preparing missionaries (this was before the age change, so there weren't as many sister missionaries either). He was as excited as I was and let me start my paperwork twelve months before my mission-age birthday instead of the customary four months before. When I found out I couldn't submit my mission application for another seven months, I was disappointed but not disheartened.

I started my new countdown, and finally my call arrived! "You are assigned to labor in the Oregon Portland Mission. You will prepare to preach the gospel in American Sign Language." Excitement, joy, amazement, and enthusiasm filled me. I cried and laughed and screamed and jumped up and down because this was the mission of my dreams! I absolutely love sign language, and outside of Utah, Oregon was my favorite place. *God loves me,* I thought. *Here we go!*

The day I had dreamed of all my life finally came. I was set apart as a full-time missionary, and the next day my parents and I headed to Provo. We pulled into the drop-off zone at the MTC, I hugged my parents and told them I loved them, and then two elders grabbed my bags and ushered me down the sidewalk. I was beyond excited, so much so that I didn't even look back at my parents. I was given my name tag, and I thought I was going to burst from joy. My picture was taken for my key card, and I don't think I have ever seen my smile that big. The next thing I knew, I was in a classroom with my district and being introduced to my companion. She was so beautiful and wonderful and was just as excited—and nervous—as I was. We were meant to be companions, and we knew it from day one.

The next couple of days were grueling. Everyone kept saying, "Just make it to Sunday; it gets so much better after Sunday." I didn't hate it, but it was long and hard and definitely immersion by fire. Sunday came, and just as everyone promised, everything suddenly seemed better. The next couple of weeks after that were all kind of a blur. Up at 6:00 A.M., breakfast, class, lunch, class, gym break, class, dinner, class, bedtime, and then repeat. Sundays were the only different days other than Tuesday nights, when we had a huge devotional with the whole MTC.

My companion and I had both studied sign language before our missions, so we had a great foundation. We studied hard, prayed hard, and laughed hard. Our signing was improving, our teaching was improving, and we were learning how to better understand the Spirit and get answers to our prayers. By week four, I had been called to be the coordinating sister, which is basically like the zone leader for the sisters in our zone. It was fantastic! We were getting to know all the other sisters in our branch, we were teaching, we were feeling the Spirit strongly and consistently, and we were receiving personal revelation left and right. Nothing could stop us. Everything was going perfectly . . . or so I thought.

On my one-month mark—to the day—my right wrist and forearm started hurting and giving me problems. My companion and I went to the MTC doctor's office, and they put me on some anti-inflammatory medication and then put my arm in a sturdy brace. I was told not to sign, not to write unless absolutely necessary, and to take it easy for the next ten days to see if this lessened my pain level.

The next week was difficult as I followed everything the doctor prescribed. I was so determined to get my right hand better that I literally did almost nothing with it. It got frustrating; I felt useless in class and in lessons because what signing I could do was limited to my left hand. Not only that, but the medication I was on wasn't agreeing with my body. Now, on top of the constant pain in my arm, I also didn't feel well. It was very difficult to concentrate and to be happy and patient.

During week seven in the MTC, things took a turn for the worse. I recorded in my journal: *Wow, today was emotional. Both of my wrists are in braces now, and I'm not allowed to sign at all (possibly [temporarily], possibly [permanently]). I got back to class having held in tears . . . my teacher asked if I was okay, and I burst into sobs! It was awful; I didn't even know what hit me.*

The doctor had told me he thought I had tendonitis in my left arm. He said I could try massage therapy; however, the MTC didn't offer that, so I would have to go home if I chose that course. I again broke down in tears. I told him that if it was at all possible, I did *not* want to go home. He said I could also go the medical route—I could have a nerve test and then surgery, an injection, or physical therapy, and still possibly go home. I was really having a hard time by this point in our conversation. He told me I should talk to my branch president and my district president, and they would help me figure things out.

My companion had to call our branch president for me because I couldn't get any words out. At this point, I was a wreck and overwhelmed with my emotions. We went into an empty classroom, and she held me as I sobbed. My heart was breaking. My soul felt as if a piece was slowly being torn from it. I didn't know what to do. I didn't want to go home, but it was looking like that was my only option.

My district president said he would call my stake president at home to inform him of the situation, see what he thought, and then have me call my parents to discuss what needed to be done. He asked if I was excited to talk to my parents and my response was, "No. Not for this conversation."

We sat and waited for a good thirty to forty-five minutes. During that time, the MTC president came and talked with me and informed me that I had been brought up in that day's health meeting. He also said he had known my grandfather and my home patriarch. We had a nice little chat, and then he said something like, "You'll be fine." After that, I had a very peaceful feeling.

I was told, depending on my healing, I might be reassigned from a signing mission to an English-speaking mission. All I could say was that I wanted to at least stay with my ASL district for the last two-and-a-half weeks at the MTC. I told my district and MTC mission leaders that I wouldn't sign. They wanted me to come back in a week and tell them how my arms were doing. If they were doing better, then we would look at my other options. If they were worse, then a decision would be made. Possibly home, possibly doctors, possibly English.

I called my mom and dad and told them everything. They were incredibly comforting and said they would support me in anything I decided. I told them, "I know the Lord has a plan for me, and I will trust in Him."

For the next week, I was extremely cautious with my arms. I didn't sign. Instead, my teachers or companion would write for me, and I did my best to get my arms better. Regardless of what I did, however, I was constantly in agony, with the pain keeping me up most nights. My companion was incredible—so patient and loving, always praying for me, helping me, and keeping me focused on what really mattered: our teaching and learning.

Another journal entry records: *Tonight I have received a little piece of revelation. I was and have been praying to know God's will for me and what I should prepare for. I got this sense of peace and calmness and the feeling I will probably be going home (hopefully for only a week). I had this thought: You have a special and important mission to fulfill. I will be with thee and you shall still serve your mission. You have borne this burden well and will continue to do so for a time . . . Be patient, and know that I am with thee.* Heavenly Father is so wonderful. For the entire time I was going through this trial, I continued to receive little pieces of revelation exactly like that, encouraging me and letting me know I was not alone and that I had a special mission. I just didn't know what that special mission was. Throughout the next few days, I talked with many people and decided I needed to fast and pray to see if going home was the right thing. So that's what I did.

The day I fasted was the day travel plans were handed out to my whole district. As soon as I looked at my travel plans, I knew I wouldn't be on that flight. I knew I needed to go home and get better. It was incredibly hard thinking about going home even though I knew it was what I was supposed to do.

The next Sunday was another difficult day. During Sacrament meeting, the bishop's counselor had me stand as he announced my release as coordinating sister. "This sweet sister's hands are in casts, and we don't know what is going to happen to her. We want to take a load off her shoulders and hope that things will be okay." I sat down in tears, unable to look at anyone. I was going home. I wasn't questioning why; I was just sad. I knew it was the will of the Lord, and I was trying to do as the Lord commanded, but there were definitely tears and heartache.

The day my parents picked me up from the MTC, I did not cry a single tear. I was sad to leave, I was sad to be going home, but I was filled with peace. That night, my stake president released me, and I had to take my name tag off. Once again I was heartbroken, but again I didn't cry. Wednesday I spent all day praying and thinking and asking what I was supposed to do now. Thursday I went to the temple and vividly received my answer. It was a very powerful and spiritual answer. I was sitting in the Celestial room praying and asking if I really was supposed to stay home, and I received the clear answer that I was.

The next few days after I left the temple were rough. Satan was working on me all weekend. I started doubting my answer, wondering if I had made it up or misinterpreted it. Then a former bishop of mine, and good family friend, talked to me. He said, "Your whole family has had peace about you coming home; that is something that wouldn't happen if it wasn't right." That same weekend another family friend approached me as well, unbidden by the first family friend, and expressed almost the exact same sentiments. This helped me a lot to finally come to peace with the answer I had received.

The next few weeks were crazy. The prompting that I wasn't to return to my mission was not the only prompting I received. I also felt that I wasn't supposed to go back to the college where I had been attending classes before my mission and that I wasn't supposed to pursue my same major. On top of it all, I also received the answer that I wasn't to marry the man I had dated before my mission and was then currently dating and thought I would marry!

For about a week I was entirely lost, confused as to why I was now home sixteen months earlier than planned, with no school, no major, and no boyfriend! But the Lord opens doors where doors had been closed. I quickly received revelation, and within two weeks I had applied to another university, with a major related to my previous one, and I had housing and a job! It had all happened very fast. Things were looking up.

The next year, however, was the most incredible and horrific emotional roller coaster of my life. Satan attacked me every chance he got. I could hardly hear of a missionary leaving or returning home without bursting into tears. Sometimes even an Oregon license plate would set me off.

Satan worked on me relentlessly. I felt like I didn't have enough faith or trust in the Lord because I was still having such a hard time with the fact that I was not on my mission. I felt as if maybe I had just given up or maybe I just wasn't cut out for the hard work and labor that is involved with a mission. Or maybe I wasn't faithful enough or spiritual enough. Thoughts like this invaded my every waking moment. I didn't know where else to turn. I had talked to my bishop, my parents, and other leaders. I had prayed and fasted, but I still felt as though I had failed the Lord.

It was especially terrible when people discovered I had served a mission. I would get really excited to tell them my story and that I experienced the most incredible things on my mission in the MTC. Then they would ask *the* question: "Where did you serve your mission?"

Awkward silence. "Well . . . I was called to the Oregon Portland mission doing sign language, but I only got to do the two months in the MTC and then had to come home because of medical problems." The reply was always the same: "Oh. I'm sorry."

Failure! It seemed they were screaming it in my face. *You didn't serve a mission, and you don't deserve the title of a returned missionary.* That's how I felt people looked at me. It was also how I felt about myself. Every. Single. Day. *How can I call myself a returned missionary or say that I served a mission when I didn't even get into the mission field?*

I felt like I had had the most amazing mission, the most spiritual experiences, the best stories, but that my mission was not acceptable as a *real* mission. I didn't have *real* investigators. I didn't teach *real* lessons. But they were all so real to me.

When I couldn't handle it any longer, I went to a therapist through LDS Family Services who specifically helps early home, medically released missionaries, which are available in some areas. I was almost ashamed to go, but I was so confused and occasionally so depressed that I didn't know what else to do. The thing that helped me most was when the therapist said, "If the prophet or even Jesus Christ Himself were standing before you right now, they would say, 'Well done, thou good and faithful servant.' Did you put your heart and soul into serving while you were there? Yes. Did you abide by the same rules as all other missionaries? Yes. Did you have that name tag bearing Christ's name? Yes. Were you serving Him every waking hour while you were out? Yes. You served a full-time mission, and don't let anyone else make you think otherwise."

My next stumbling block was that I was afraid. Afraid that all those blessings that my family had been promised would now not apply to them. My family was going through a really rough time because the economy had plummeted and our finances had taken a hard blow, not to mention the other personal struggles each member of my family was facing. My mission was supposed to be blessing them, so now what was going to happen? The thought inside my mind said I had failed my family. I wasn't strong enough to stay. I wasn't faithful enough to stay.

Nothing seemed important enough for me to have come home from my mission. And nothing seemed to be helping. I read my scriptures, said my prayers, and went to the temple weekly or more. I read talks and quotes, listened to inspirational music, focused on school and work, but I just never felt like I was doing enough.

Once again, the therapist gave light to my dark web of endless thoughts. "Look at how many family members you have been able to talk to, love, and touch by just living your testimony. Maybe your mission was to help someone or multiple people in the MTC and now the Lord needs you here helping your family and friends, those who mean the most to you, to stay on the right path. To help *them* so they don't lose their way or so they can see the light and love that radiates from you and come to the gospel. Your mission is different from others' missions. Try to look back on the things you have accomplished and look forward to what the Lord wants you to do."

Slowly but surely I started realizing all the things I would have missed or things I would not have experienced without this difficult change in my life. I realized I do not see the whole picture, but the Lord does. Maybe I had experienced what I had experienced so that when I met someone else who had gone through a similar situation, I could succor them. Maybe it was to make me stronger or to test just how much I would do to follow my Lord and Savior.

I then remembered all the times I had received personal revelation about how the Lord had a special mission for me and all the peace I felt at coming home and receiving my answer. I realized the Lord did indeed have a work and a purpose for me and that focusing on the negative was only inhibiting me from seeing and doing the work the Lord had for me here at home.

I noticed that sometimes I was looking so longingly at what might have been that I was missing what might *be*. I was missing my true mission, which was and is in everyday life! My situation was similar to the dilemma explained by Alexander Graham Bell: "When one door closes, another door opens, but we so often look so long and so regretfully upon the closed door that we do not see the ones which open for us."[10]

I am still not entirely sure why I had to come home and why I had to stay home. I know this much, though: as soon as I accepted Heavenly Father's answer to me to stay home and started working to find a new school, the pain in my arms, which had been constant and agonizing for more than a month, simply disappeared. The Lord knew exactly what needed to happen so that I would come home, but then once I was on the path He had planned for me, He relieved me of that pain and has been opening doors for me ever since. I know that, in time (maybe in the next life), I will understand more clearly why things happened the way they happened, but until then, I trust that the Lord has a mission and a plan for me and that He will lead me *if* I allow him to.

I'm not perfect, and I still have moments of longing and sadness, but it no longer runs my life or overwhelms it. The Lord is good and has given us so many opportunities; sometimes we just have to open our eyes to see those He has put right before us. Rely on the Lord. *Trust* in the Lord and in His timing as well.

---

10 Quoted in Jonathan J. Doll, "OPEN DOORS PART ONE: When One Door Closes, Another Door Opens," *Huffpost*, accessed December 12, 2017, https://www.huffingtonpost.com/entry/open-doors-part-one-when-one-door-closes-another_us_58e693f4e4b0d6001f07f2c1, Apr. 6, 2017.

I know everything happens for a reason. I know Heavenly Father and Jesus Christ know us perfectly. I know They love us perfectly and infinitely. I know this is the true gospel and that it is a gospel of joy and peace and love. I love my Savior and my Redeemer. I hope that if you are reading this you have found some bit of revelation or peace to help you. Life is good and beautiful. Although I am not set apart as a missionary anymore, I have taken Elder Neil L. Andersen's words to heart and have painted my nametag on my heart.[11] You are always called; you are always doing the Lord's work. Press on, press on.

11 See Neil L. Andersen, "It's a Miracle," *Ensign*, May 2013.

CHAPTER 10
THAT BIG LOVE
BY AVERY BARNES

"For I am persuaded, that neither death, nor life, nor angels, nor principalities, nor powers, nor things present, nor things to come, [n]or height, nor depth, nor any other creature, shall be able to separate us from the love of God, which is in Christ Jesus our Lord." (Romans 8:38–39)

The beginning of one's mission is a well-worn story, one everyone knows. You receive the letter (or, email, as it is nowadays) and prepare to read the anticipated words stating where you will spend the next year and a half or two years. Family and loved ones gather with bated breath and blank minds because, out of all the options of where you could go, the choice you've made to be a missionary outshines everything else, and the details fall into place. You begin reading and soon find out when and where this crazy adventure is going to take place. As I did, you may think yourself crazy as it all sinks in: Can I actually do this? Although many young adults share similar first steps in their mission journeys, our paths to the mission-call opening and the experiences that follow are unique. No two missionary stories are the same. And I'm here to tell you mine.

I was eight when I attended church for the first time, and I was eight when I was baptized into The Church of Jesus Christ of Latter-day Saints. My decision had come after feeling the warmth of the people in my ward and the light that comes with personal revelation. I am the oldest of three siblings, and I am blessed to have extremely supportive parents. My mother grew up in the Church and started attending worship services again around this same time. My father's family wasn't particularly religious, but growing up in the Bible Belt of Tennessee had led to a fair amount of religious exposure.

I remember very vividly the fear I felt when telling members of my family I had decided to be baptized. This wasn't because I feared rejection or discouragement but because I knew the significance of what I was about to do. Church would not simply be a social and spiritual uplift but would become a commitment and a community. The missionaries came over and shared the lessons with me. When they spoke, I felt the Spirit's sweet confirmation of my decision. I made many friends in Primary and loved singing the songs about what we did in the summertime and trying to be like Jesus. These friends and basic gospel principles are what propelled me to come back every Sunday and eventually to participate in weekday activities, which led to four years of seminary, which in turn led to my decision to attend Brigham Young University (BYU) in pursuit of higher education.

After I learned that girls could serve missions too, the Spirit gently opened my heart to the idea, and it was something I always had in the back of my mind. Later, when the age requirement lowered from twenty-one to nineteen years, this idea of serving a mission seemed to become more of a reality, as it did for many young women at the time. Seeing other sister missionaries return from their missions made my heart buzz, and that could only mean one thing: this whole mission thing might be for me. Now, this prospect wasn't actively discouraged in my house, but my parents had made it clear how sorely they would miss me if I chose that path. As the oldest child, I felt it was my responsibility to maintain some semblance of our family structure in any way I could, and leaving on a mission seemed to be expressly against that. However, I still couldn't shake the feeling that it was something my Heavenly Father wanted me to do. So, after a year of college, my missionary application was sent in, and I received my call.

"Sister Barnes, you are hereby called to serve in the Italy Rome Mission." I was floored. Never once had I considered Italy as a place to serve, but the thought electrified me and kept me going through the long months of waiting that I spent before leaving. Those months seemed dark and monotonous at times. I yearned for the mission experience I saw on my horizon.

Ever since I was young, I have had an affinity for love and romance stories. I pined for a true love's kiss between prince and princess, envied the enemies-turned-lovers stories, and even yearned for the convoluted emotions of a love triangle. While the love I now craved wasn't a romantic love, I burned with a desire to share my heart with the people of Italy. I felt I had so much love to give, and those lonely months of waiting became a trial of their own. The extended time I was able to spend with my family was a silver lining that I will be forever grateful for. But I felt there was a big love out there for me, something that would fill my soul so fully that it seemed my skin would not be able to contain it. I knew my mission would be one of love, but I never expected that love to be so immense.

Each individual's mission experience is so unique because it depends on so many different factors. Our experiences are colored by who our companions are, where we go, when we go, and how we've prepared. When I left on my mission, nothing could have prepared me for the heartbreak of saying goodbye to my family. It stung so badly that I pushed the pain deep down and tried to continue in faith. My faith that Heavenly Father was preparing people to hear my testimony was the thought that kept me going through life at the MTC. I have many fond memories there, but spending Christmas in the MTC and being so close to where I had just spent two amazing semesters at BYU was more challenging than I thought it would be.

My relief came when we all boarded the plane and flew off to be "wanderers in a strange land" (Alma 13:23). After arriving, the unfamiliarity of Italy filled the holes in my heart in a lot of ways. I didn't have enough time during the day to be homesick when there was an entire language to learn, cities to explore, and people to meet. Mornings, on the other hand, were hard—especially in the beginning. The thought of the timeline ahead of me was crushing, and it was all I could do to roll out of bed onto my knees each day and say a prayer. These intimate daily prayers became my rock, my helpline, and my solace when life seemed too great to bear. During my mission, I watched the general conference where Elder Kyle S. McKay spoke of the immediate goodness of God. He testified that "[t]he immediate goodness of God comes to all who call upon Him with real intent and full purpose of heart. This includes those who cry out in earnest desperation, when deliverance seems so distant and suffering seems prolonged, even intensified."[24] I felt His immediate goodness sustain me every time I kneeled to pray. Every time. More often than not, my problem wasn't solved, nor was an answer received, but I was given the strength to keep going when I thought I no longer could.

As time passed, my confidence grew and many aspects of mission life that I had initially dreaded became enjoyable. I loved talking and connecting with members of the Church. Conversations on the bus no longer seemed like a hostage situation but an opportunity to make a real human connection. That big love I had lived for began to fill my heart.

I had the opportunity to serve in the Rome Italy Temple Visitors' Center for a period of time as well. This portion of my mission changed my life in a very specific way. My testimony of the temple grew astronomically during my

---

24 Kyle S. McKay, "The Immediate Goodness of God," *Ensign*, May 2019, 105.

service there. I gained a deep and abiding love for the precious promises we make in temples and the sacred spirit that can be found within those walls. Living now, in a time when regular temple attendance isn't an option due to the COVID-19 pandemic, I am so grateful for the time I got to be even in the vicinity of the Lord's house and for the opportunity to know and feel the power of holy places.

Eventually, I did have to leave the sanctuary of the temple grounds, but I was always able to bring that spirit with me wherever I went. The last area I was called to serve in was the island country of Malta, a little spit of land off the coast of Sicily. Hardly anyone in the mission got called there, but I was blessed enough to meet and love the Maltese saints. Everyone will tell you that a mission is all about the people, and nowhere was that truer than in Malta. In its small branch, we were all each other had. And in a very Grinchlike fashion, it felt like my heart grew three sizes during my time there.[25]

However, in a matter of days, all of our hopes and dreams for the island and its branch of saints came crashing down as we received the call to evacuate because of the spread of coronavirus. The Church had recently changed its policies about which missionaries could remain serving in their mission areas and which ones would be sent home or reassigned to new locations in efforts to keep everyone safe from the virus. Although the majority of people in my mission were directed to quarantine in the areas they were currently in, my companion was told she would be going home because she was already nearing the end of her mission. We were the only sister missionaries in our area, and if travel hadn't been so restricted, a sister serving in Italy could have transferred to Malta to be my new companion, or I could have returned to Italy to join missionaries there. But COVID-19 had impacted the surrounding areas so greatly that that simply wasn't an option. I felt my heart shatter as our mission president relayed the news that we could no longer stay. We would both be leaving our mission immediately. I was supposed to have spent three more months on that blessed island. It wasn't fair to me, and it wasn't fair to them. I was crushed.

All it took was the passage of about twenty-four hours and a frenzy of packing and cleaning for what felt like the entirety of my mission to be condensed into sticky notes, which we gave the elders who were staying behind. It felt unfinished, and my mind rebelled at the thought that this was going to be how I would end my mission. I was supposed to share my departure testimony and have a final interview with my mission president, or at least give a homecoming talk in church when I arrived home, to provide some semblance of closure. Instead, there were masks and quarantines, with little clarity as to what

25 Dr. Seuss, *How the Grinch Stole Christmas*, 1957.

the future would hold. It was all I could do on the flight home not to lose my composure completely.

Throughout my mission, I told everyone who asked about my post-mission plans that after my allotted eighteen months of service, I would return to "normal life." Instead, what I came back to was anything but normal. With no religious expectations in my home, I have come from the most enlightening experience in my life to a situation of little to no spiritual support from anyone other than myself. For a while, I thought everything was fine, and I was just so relieved to be back with my family that I ignored the lack of the Spirit in my new life. Personal study seemed stale with no one to share it with, and praying right as I awoke in the morning was soon replaced by checking what I had missed on my phone. These are easily fixable problems, but my denial made it hard to even admit that they were problems. I can see now that it was all an attempt to ignore the heartbreak that coming home early had caused. My mission had given me all I wanted and more, but that had all vanished before I could even comprehend the gravity of what had happened. I was looking for my big love, but the process had broken my heart.

As I have been nursing this heartbreak, I have come to realize that this was all part of my Heavenly Father's plan for me. I was supposed to come home three months early during a global pandemic. The normal fanfare of finishing a mission wasn't a part of my plan; rather, being able to be home and support my family was. My Heavenly Father wanted me to feel the hurt of losing something I loved so dearly because it was the only way I could truly see its worth. And I wasn't left helpless in this hurt. As I'd learned on my mission, there was always the immediate goodness of God's Son—my Savior and Redeemer, Jesus Christ—to shed light on me whenever life felt too dark. I have been reminded that the dark times are always purposeful.

One of my favorite speakers, Sister Francine R. Bennion, spoke on this topic of finding purpose in suffering. She writes,

> We suffer because we were willing to pay the cost of *being* and of being here with others in their ignorance and inexperience as well as our own . . . Like Christ in the desert, we did not ask God to let us try falling or being bruised only on condition that he catch us before we touch ground and save us from real hurt. We were willing to *know* hurt.[26]

---

26 Francine R. Bennion, "A Latter-day Saint Theology of Suffering" in *A Heritage of Faith: Talks Selected from the BYU Women's Conferences*, ed. Mary E. Stovall and Carol Cornwall Madsen (Salt Lake City: Deseret Book, 1988), 53–76. Used by permission of Deseret

Although the hurt caused by my sudden and unexpected goodbye to my big love was profound, it has allowed me to know Christ more deeply. The immediate goodness of God has sustained me both on and off the mission and has opened my heart more fully to Christ's continuous love, which is the biggest love of all.

Know the hurt; lean in to it. In doing so we can become more like our Savior and fulfill one of our purposes here on Earth. He can heal our hearts through His love. Armed with the knowledge that there is opposition in all things, we can embrace the exquisite pain of mortality knowing that even greater joy is available through and because of Him who felt it all, even Jesus Christ.

Book Company.

CHAPTER 11
PAINTED ON YOUR HEART
BY COLE HENDRICKS (PSEUDONYM)

"Wherefore, ye must press forward with a steadfastness in Christ, having a perfect brightness of hope, and a love of God and of all men. Wherefore, if ye shall press forward, feasting upon the word of Christ, and endure to the end, behold, thus saith the Father: Ye shall have eternal life." (2 Nephi 31:20)

Elder Neil L. Andersen of the Twelve Apostles gave a general conference talk entitled, "It's a Miracle." He said, "If you're not a full-time missionary with a missionary badge pinned on your coat, now is the time to paint one on your heart—painted, as Paul said, 'not with ink, but with the Spirit of the living God.' . . . All of us have a contribution to make to this miracle."[19]

If there's anything I love, it's miracles. And Elder Andersen said that we *each* have a contribution to make to the miracle of missionary work going on right now. Our lives fit perfectly together to accomplish God's work and glory. And it really is a miracle. I love what Elder Andersen says about painting a missionary badge—and therefore Christ's name—on our hearts.

I was in the MTC during the general conference when President Thomas S. Monson announced the age change for missionaries. I can't describe in words the excitement and energy in the air at the MTC and in each of our hearts. The enthusiasm everyone felt was almost tangible. We ate up stories from the outside world about eighteen-, nineteen-, and twenty-year-olds filling up doctor's offices so they could submit their papers as soon as possible. Our leaders and MTC speakers testified to each of us that we were called on a mission at this specific time to be a part of this miracle.

Three weeks before I was scheduled to leave the MTC, I suddenly got really sick. The doctors weren't sure what I had, but it felt as though my body just shut down. I had to sleep for about fifteen hours a day, my muscles constantly

19 Neil L. Andersen, "It's a Miracle," *Ensign*, May 2013, 78.

felt as if I'd sprinted for miles, and mentally I felt like it was three A.M. all the time. I was just so out of it. I took it easy for the first couple of days, hoping to sleep it off so that I could get back to work as soon as I could. But those days started adding up without any change in my health, despite the many prayers and fasts offered by missionaries and leaders in the MTC and from family at home.

I remember lying in one of the beds at the MTC doctor's office day after day (I became kind of a frequent flyer there) and thinking, *What kind of a missionary am I?* I thought about the stress I was putting on my companion from the burden I felt I'd become, about the language that I should be learning and the doctrine I should be studying. I wanted nothing more than to be a diligent and obedient missionary, yet there I was, sleeping my life away and having very limited energy to study.

That bed in the doctor's office became a sacred place to me as I contemplated what it really meant to be a good missionary. Soon those verb tenses and conjugations seemed less and less important. Language study is definitely a valuable part of missionary work, but it didn't define me while I was sick. At that point, we still thought I'd either get better in time to go with my group or maybe have to stay at the MTC a little longer until I was well enough to go. I realized Heavenly Father must need me to go through this experience for some reason but that I could still be a missionary by representing Christ—even if I was just a representative alone in that little curtained-off room. I could still show Christ I loved Him by what was in my heart, because I didn't have the strength to show it by my actions. My missionary tag, with Christ's name on it, became more sacred as I internalized these thoughts.

After being sick for two weeks, I seemed to start feeling better in answer to everyone's prayers and fasting. But the Lord had a different plan for me. Three days before my scheduled flight, I found myself alone and as sick as ever on a plane headed for home.

I'd always heard missionaries have an emotional time taking their name tag off after their mission, but I could never have imagined how hard it would be for me to take mine off so soon and so suddenly. After all, this was the dream the Lord had given me and that I had trusted in and loved so much.

It was difficult for me to hear talks or discussions on missionary work or anything about the missionary age change. Although I knew with all my heart that the Lord had a bigger plan for me, I felt I'd been kicked off His team. To complicate the situation, I wanted so badly to go back on my mission as soon as I was better, but for some reason it just didn't feel right and even though it took me months even to verbalize these promptings (and I hoped that they were wrong), I knew deep down I was home for good. It broke my heart. I had gone from being involved in the greatest work this world has ever known at one of the most exciting times to be a part of it to lying in bed at home alone all day for months. And this time without my name tag.

I was unprepared for the ways Satan would attack me when I came home. Thoughts that in my head I knew were lies planted themselves deep within my heart. They came in all forms, including overwhelming feelings of unworthiness and worthlessness. I had not only come home early from my mission and felt that I was letting down my family, other missionaries, myself, and, worst of all, God but I also had no contribution to make at home either.

I had planned on and wanted so badly to be serving God as a full-time missionary during the very time I was now wasting. Instead of spending all my energy devoted to finding Heavenly Father's children to teach and inviting them to come unto Christ, I now spent what little energy I had in five-minute scripture studies, mostly just staring at the page because I felt so dizzy. Rather than lifting others and helping them come to church, I was only able to make it to about twenty minutes of sacrament meeting every other week. The value of my life felt like it had plummeted and that I had fallen hard. I felt like a nothing.

Amid the often unseen hurt I experienced and continued to struggle with for years, the Lord has poured down blessings and tender mercies. I felt I could say with the prophet Ammon from the Book of Mormon, "Yea, I know that I am nothing; as to my strength I am weak; therefore I will not boast of myself, but I will boast of my God, for in his strength I can do all things" (Alma 26:12). Even though my strength was weak, I knew God had a plan for me and that He could see a bigger picture than I could. He was now calling me to a different mission in life.

As months passed with no improvement with my health, a good friend asked me what lessons I was learning while being sick. I responded, "Heavenly Father is teaching me a lot right now. The main thing I have learned is that He still loves and values me and my service, even though it seems so insignificant. I think I had fallen into an unknown trap of thinking my worth depended on what I was doing or the accomplishments I made, rather than the sole fact that I am a child of God. Nothing can change that. Heavenly Father will always love me because I am His child."

I reflect on the MTC often. I had no idea, of course, when going to the MTC, that my entire full-time mission would be on its grounds. For me, it is far more than a layover to a final destination or even just a place of fond memories and spiritual growth. The MTC is sacred. It is the place where I walked with the Savior's name printed on a badge over my heart. I loved the fact that the people I met there knew me as a missionary.

I was supposed to meet the amazing leaders and missionaries at the MTC with whom I served, and I needed the training I received there. But I would never go to the mission area to where I was called. My mission field would be somewhere else. It would be different but not inferior.

Although the pain I felt in losing my mission was much deeper than I could have ever imagined, I know that in God's strength, I can do all things. I knew that He would heal me eventually. I knew He cared about me and heard my cries when the pain was more than I could take. I knew He would, in this life or the next, fulfill every promised blessing I'd received about serving those people. And I trust that He is again leading me to new dreams.

During the time I wore a missionary badge, as well as the time since coming home, I held the following lyrics of one of my favorite hymns close to my heart:

> Savior, Redeemer of my soul,
> Whose mighty hand hath made me whole,
> Whose wondrous pow'r hath raised me up
> And filled with sweet my bitter cup!
> What tongue my gratitude can tell,
> O gracious God of Israel. . . .
> Never can I repay thee, Lord,
> But I can love thee. Thy pure word,
> Hath it not been my one delight,
> My joy by day, my dream by night?
> Then let my lips proclaim it still,
> And all my life reflect thy will.[20]

Even though for months I spent my days physically alone, Christ *never* left me alone. I felt the power of the Atonement of Jesus Christ strengthen my Spirit beyond my own capacity.

When I was serving Christ, with His name on my badge, and now that I am striving to paint it onto my heart, I have felt His love. When we act under the influence of the Spirit, we *are* representing Christ and painting His name

---

20 "Savior, Redeemer of My Soul," *Hymns*, 112.

onto our hearts. We paint this badge on when we pray for ways to serve others and when we move forward trusting that God will guide our steps. As we do these things, Heavenly Father *will* help us fulfill all of our dreams. He will bless us more than we can now comprehend.

I can feel His hand helping make me whole physically, emotionally, and spiritually. He has filled my life with tender mercies I can't even count and, in doing so, filled, as the "Savior, Redeemer of My Soul" hymn teaches, with sweet my bitter cup. I know He will fill with sweet *your* bitter cup as well.

We can never repay our Savior, but we can love Him. This gospel really is my joy by day and my dream by night. I know that as we let our lips proclaim it still and live our lives to reflect His will, God will be our strength *wherever* we are called to serve our King.[21]

21 See "Called to Serve," *Hymns*, 174.

CHAPTER 12
TRUST IN THE LORD
BY AUSTIN WALZ

"Trust in the Lord with all thine heart; and lean not unto thine own understanding. In all thy ways acknowledge him, and he shall direct thy paths." *(Prov. 3:5–6)*

My companion and I were sitting at our desks after dinner one night around eight thirty when the phone rang. I had no idea what was about to come. We had been in self-isolation for three days for protection from COVID-19 as directed by our mission president, trying to do as much remote teaching and proselytizing as we could during that time. I was bored, lonely, tired, and depressed. But those feelings paled in comparison to the emotions I was about to experience. I was already having a rough time, and the call I received from my mission president didn't help at all.

When I answered the phone, he asked to speak to me in private.

"Elder Walz, you probably weren't expecting a call from me tonight," he said. "I'm calling because when you put in your missionary application, you filled out a section saying that you have a history of asthma, correct?"

Worry and anxiety began rising within me as he spoke. "Yes sir, I did," I replied.

"Well, unfortunately, the Missionary Department in Salt Lake has directed that all missionaries who have certain medical conditions are to be sent home to their families."

My heart dropped. At that moment, I was standing in the kitchen across from my companion, and I felt I needed to get out, to go somewhere else, so I ran upstairs to my bedroom closet and closed the door behind me. I could feel the tears coming.

He said there was a 99.9% chance I'd be sent home but that he would try his best to keep me in the mission field longer. I tried to reason with him, telling him I hadn't had to use an inhaler for years, but my mission president explained that the Missionary Department was very adamant that anyone with any vulnerability to the coronavirus needed to be sent home. He gave me permission to call my family and tell them the news that night.

Before I made the call, I took a few moments to take it all in. I was being sent home. I had only about seven months left to go to complete my anticipated two-year mission, and I so desperately wanted to stay. But, unexpectedly, it was now my time to go. God had other plans for me.

The shock lasted for the next few days. I had about two weeks before I was scheduled to go home, and all day every day until then to think about it. It felt like a dream, like some vivid hallucination that wasn't real. I had expected to be out for two years. And now that had all changed in a second. I didn't believe it at first. I didn't want to believe it. My mission president had said he was sending me home on April 1, and it all seemed like some sort of April Fools' joke. But it wasn't.

After the shock faded somewhat, the disappointment hit like a wave. Sleep became rare as I lay awake at night thinking of all the things I'd done on the mission and all the things I wish I could have done. I lost any remaining motivation I had, and in between online proselytizing appointments, my days were spent thinking about all the might-have-beens and what-ifs of my mission. I wished with all my heart that I could continue to serve. I even tried to bargain with God, asking and pleading to stay out longer. During this time, I clung to the 0.1% chance that I could stay out, hoping that if I prayed harder and read my scriptures more that God would change His mind. After a few days of unanswered pleadings and seemingly unproductive scripture study sessions, I fell into a deeper pit of depression. I felt God was ignoring me, like He didn't want to listen to me anymore.

As days continued to pass, I tried to think more positively. I started looking to the future instead of the past. I prayed again, but this time submitting my will to Heavenly Father's. I tried to think about what Jesus would do in this position, and I reminded myself of when He was in the Garden of Gethsemane. For a moment, He didn't want to follow through with the Atonement if there were any other way to do it, but He ultimately took that difficult path and submitted His will to the Father's. In doing so, He followed through with God's plan and provided salvation to all mankind. I was then reminded of when I first left on my mission. I didn't know what I was doing, what to expect, or what would happen. But I knew that a mission was what the Lord wanted me to do, and I had made a promise to myself that, no matter what happened, I would follow the guidance of the Lord and do all He asked of me. I figured that submitting my will to His in this situation was a part of that promise. I needed to trust in Him, as I had done for the past seventeen months. He knew me, He was aware of me, and He had a way prepared for me.

I continued to pray and ask for strength to overcome the obstacles placed in front of me, and I continued to study the scriptures. This time I searched them for answers from God, not just the ones I wanted. While doing so, I came across D&C 126. Although it is a very short section, it spoke volumes to me. It states:

> Dear and well-beloved brother, Brigham Young, verily thus saith the Lord unto you: My servant Brigham, it is no more required at your hand to leave your family as in times past, for your offering is acceptable to me.
>
> I have seen your labor and toil in journeyings for my name.
>
> I therefore command you to send my word abroad, and take especial care of your family from this time, henceforth and forever. Amen. (D&C 126:1–3)

When I read these words, I felt like my mind was opened. I had a specific reason to go home. I may not know that reason now, but I know that God knows. And, just like Brigham Young, I needed to allow God to guide me through it and do what He needs me to do. I knew that my time spent in the Lord's service was not wasted and that it was no longer required that I be away from my family.

As time went on, I found that I no longer worried about what I could have done over the next seven months. Instead, I thought about the new possibilities, potential, and plan God had for me. I felt like I was starting to crawl out of the deep pit of depression into the light that comes from hope in Jesus Christ.

Once I had come to terms with the fact that I was going home, I started to look forward to it. I no longer dreaded it. I could finally be with my family again and hang out with my friends. I could do the things I missed. I realized it wasn't all bad. In every bad situation, you can find something to be happy about.

At this point, I had about a week left until April 1, and I didn't think I could handle being stuck in our apartment much longer. There wasn't much to do, and time seemed to go by so slowly. My companion and I tried to pass the time by talking about all sorts of topics, which helped keep my mind busy instead of counting down the hours until I could go home. Eventually, I found that being inside all day wasn't all bad. I was finally able to cope and deal with all the feelings I had been struggling with. I opened up to my companion and other missionaries. I spoke with my mission president, and he helped me to feel accomplished and to view my mission experience as a positive one.

With about six days left to go, I decided it would be a good idea to begin packing and organizing my things. I had barely finished getting ready for the day when we received a phone call from the mission office. They said it was urgent that I respond immediately. There was a mix-up with the flight plans for all the missionaries in the mission who were being sent home due to the coronavirus. Instead of leaving on April 1, we were to board the plane that day at twelve p.m. I no longer had the luxury of organizing my belongings ahead of time, as I had initially planned to do that day. I quickly ran to my closet, threw my clothes into my suitcase, and packed up everything I could fit.

It was then about eleven a.m., and the Atlanta Airport, where we were scheduled to depart, was an hour away from us. I was stressed out of my mind, and I remember almost having a mental breakdown on the way there. I thought about all the people I wanted to say goodbye to and see at least one more time before I left. Another wave of sadness washed over me. I had been waiting for this day for the past week, and suddenly it was right at my feet. I felt like I had no control and that I was being swept away. It was like I was simply disappearing from the mission. I didn't have much time to tell anyone other than my family that I was leaving for home. I was leaving without a goodbye to the people in the mission field I had grown to love. And that hurt more than anything.

When we arrived at the airport, we were greeted by the mission president and his wife, who were handing out gloves and masks along with our plane tickets. They wished us well and sent us on our way. After all the hustle and bustle of airport security and traveling to my gate, I sat down and looked through the window at the plane waiting for me outside of the terminal. It was a four-hour flight home, and I knew it would be the longest four hours of my life.

While waiting to board, I sat next to several other missionaries from my mission and surrounding missions, who were also waiting for their flights home. I knew a lot of these missionaries, and it felt good to be able to talk to them and have someone to relate to. It helped me realize I was not the only one experiencing this. I didn't have to go through it alone. A lot of people I knew were going through very similar things. Looking back now, I had no idea at the time how many of my friends were also coming home early from their missions. God didn't make me go through this alone. He prepared a way for me to be able to relate to others so that we could strengthen and uplift one another.

Not once since coming home have I felt unsupported by my family and friends. Every person I've spoken to and opened up to has been supportive and helpful to me and my situation. I've learned to trust others and reach out to them for help. They have really made a difference in overcoming this obstacle.

After returning home, I wasn't prepared for what came next: nothing. I had no clue what to do. I had no set plan. Because of the extremely short notice of my arrival, none of my belongings were pulled out of storage yet. I still had things in my mission field that needed to be mailed home to me. I felt like both my room and my life were being thrown together at the last minute. It was just me and my luggage and nothing to do. That was the toughest part—finding something meaningful to work toward. At least, it was for me. Before I left on my mission, I had a general idea of what I wanted to do once I came home. But when I actually returned, those plans I had set in place fell through. I know, however, that there is a reason God has me here right now, so I am determined to find my purpose. And I don't have to do it alone. I have friends, family, and most importantly, God to turn to for help. I know I can do hard things because my Savior Jesus Christ has done the hardest thing for me through His Atonement. He knows me. He knows my pain and my heartbreak, and He also knows how to heal me. So, with this knowledge, I put my trust in Him and take the next step forward.

I miss my mission and wish I could have stayed for two years. But I know I finished what God needed me to do. The mission was hard, and leaving was even harder, yet I know I can always look back on fond memories from my missionary service and be happy with the work I did for the Lord during that time. Now I am happy to move forward, and I am genuinely excited for my next stage in life.

CHAPTER 13
ANGELS ROUND ABOUT YOU
BY BRE COOPER (PSEUDONYM)

"I will not leave you comfortless: I will come to you." (John 14:18)

IMAGINE YOU JUST FINISHED RUNNING a few warm-up laps before a crucial race, after making every possible preparation during months of training. Family and friends fill the stadium to cheer you on, while butterflies of nervousness and excitement fill your body. Just as you finish your final warm-up lap, an official pulls you to the side, thanks you for your efforts, and asks you to leave. Confused, you grab your things. Then the official calls the very teammates you trained with to the starting line for the race.

What's wrong with me? you ask yourself. *Are they confused? Am I confused?* But it's too late—the race has already started. You're not sure what exactly happened, but you do know that you weren't wanted or needed, and you're walking away from your dreams—without your coach, without the fans, and without your teammates.

I hadn't planned on being done with my mission so soon. I was standing in the MTC doctor's office hearing that I would likely be going home. It was a painful blow. I stood there in the dust as I watched others run the race I was supposed to be a part of.

I'm pretty sure my companion was an angel. My body had started giving out, leaving me to feel physically and emotionally depleted throughout the demands of the day. Back at our room, she just let me cry to her, and she cried with me. I told her about my bewilderment with the whole situation. I felt disoriented and didn't understand what Heavenly Father wanted of me. My eyes grew redder and puffier as I tried to explain just how much I didn't want to go home. Neither of us knew for sure what Heavenly Father was doing with my life.

My companion didn't have answers, but she had love.

Over and over again, she told me that if I did go home because of my sickness, it wasn't because I lacked faith or because I gave up. She told me that Satan and sometimes other people would tell me I had failed and wasn't good enough. She testified that Heavenly Father would be at work in my life. She also reminded me of all the missionaries and leaders in the entire zone praying and fasting for me and that God definitely heard all of our prayers. If I was sent home, it was not because of our lack of faith, but because it was God's will.

She showed Christlike love as she testified to me of my eternal value and the good I'd done on my mission. As we wept together, I felt Heavenly Father's love encircle us, despite the overwhelming uncertainty of my future.

I have no idea why I was blessed with such an amazing companion. I know that not everyone who is sick on their mission has someone so understanding, although I pray they do. My companion had so many opportunities to be rotten to me but didn't take any of them. I know it had to be a conscious decision on her part because no one wants a sick companion, and it's definitely not easy. She missed classes at crucial times so she could help take care of me. We also didn't know if or how contagious I was at that point, and by spending so much time with me, as companions do, she risked getting sick herself. But she did as the Savior would have done and never complained. Her decision to love me and serve me so selflessly when she could have reacted in different ways has led to a friendship I cherish deeply. I will be forever grateful for such an angel in the midst of a hard time. Her example changed how I look at others.

On my flight home I cried to Heavenly Father, pleading for help. I told Him I didn't think I could get off the plane and face my family. As kind and loving as they are, I was still mortified. I got the inspiration to just think about my one-year-old niece. She became my one happy thought that got me through. I could get off the plane for her. Everything would be okay if I could just see and hold her.

I held on to that thought as I fell asleep on the plane and then again as I walked to my family. As I came into view, my niece excitedly wriggled out of my brother's arms onto the floor to crawl over to me. My brother told me later that more often than not she would seem indifferent when she saw a family member she hadn't seen for a while. Only a loving Heavenly Father and Savior could have known how much I needed that welcome from her. My sweet niece acted as my angel that day.

Other angels and tender mercies from a loving Savior carried me home and through one of the hardest times of my life. The Holy Ghost filled me with comfort and gave me the emotional and spiritual strength to face the coming days. I knew they would be difficult, but a perfect Father in Heaven gave me small, personal witnesses that these heartbreaking events were from God and that everything would ultimately work out.

As the weeks passed, I just felt so empty and lonely. I missed everything about my mission. I prayed for just one phone call, one letter, one *something* to remind me that other people still cared about me. One day a box from Amazon arrived for me. I thought it was part of a shipment I had ordered. I was surprised to see a beautiful children's book of *The Night Before Christmas* with a CD, from my elementary school music teacher. She had heard I was sick and sent me that gift with the sweetest get-well note. I bawled—the timing couldn't have been more inspired.

After getting laid off from a job, people often have feelings of worthlessness and question their abilities. Coming home early from a mission, even when you are honorably released, feels like you have been laid off—but from the greatest job you could ever do in your life. And it feels like Heavenly Father Himself is the one telling you you're not needed anymore.

In my heart I believed He really did need me, just in another location. I clung to that feeling and hoped it was real. I often prayed for strength and guidance, but usually ended up crying, and the only words that made it out were, "I'm sorry. I'm so sorry." I didn't know how I could have gotten so far off track or how I could have done something so wrong, and I hoped to be forgiven for not doing the things I was called to do. I knew logically it was flawed thinking because the situation wasn't my fault, and I hated that I was having such a difficult time.

A constant battle raged in my mind and heart between me, Heavenly Father, and Satan. Satan has a heyday with missionaries coming home early and cuts straight through to their self-worth. He immediately plants lies deep within their soul, mostly revolving around the fact that they are now a lower-class citizen in God's kingdom because it's taboo to come home early from a mission. They suddenly go from the hero sibling, friend, ward member, or cousin serving a mission to feeling like the bad egg with a defect. At least that's what Satan would have them believe, but it is not true. God loves all of us. As we strive to feel God's love for us through the Spirit, it's crucial to change the way we calculate our value. God does not and will not forget our labors of love, both on and off our mission. President Thomas S. Monson shared this measuring stick for self-worth:

> Your Heavenly Father loves you—each of you. That love never changes. It is not influenced by your appearance, by your possessions, or by the amount of money you have in your bank

> account. It is not changed by your talents and abilities. It is simply there. It is there for you when you are sad or happy, discouraged or hopeful. God's love is there for you whether or not you feel you deserve love. It is simply always there.[16]

Heavenly Father loves you because you are His child. You can't do *anything* to take that love away. Your mission did not change His love for you, and He loves the service you gave in the name of His Son, Jesus Christ. But, even if coming home early was in some way wrong, would He not still heal us? Would He not want to run to us, to reach out in love and bring us, His children, back to Him? God always invites and always loves. Nothing we do will cause our Father in Heaven or our Savior to stop loving us. That truth is eternally fixed. He does not leave us in the dust.

It may be tempting to focus on what you *didn't* do on your mission. Heavenly Father doesn't want us to do that to ourselves. Instead, He guides us to look to others who will help us see our true selves.

Elder Jeffrey R. Holland of the Quorum of the Twelve spoke about the amazing ability to love and carry one another's burdens when he said:

> Indeed heaven never seems closer than when we see the love of God manifested in the kindness and devotion of people so good and so pure that *angelic* is the only word that comes to mind. . . . My beloved brothers and sisters, I testify of angels, both the heavenly and the mortal kind. In doing so I am testifying that God never leaves us alone, never leaves us unaided in the challenges that we face. . . . On occasions, global or personal, we may feel we are distanced from God, shut out from heaven, lost, alone in dark and dreary places. Often enough that distress can be of our own making, but even then the Father of us all is watching and assisting. And always there are those angels who come and go all around us, seen and unseen, known and unknown, mortal and immortal.[17]

I determined to surround myself with those who saw the good in me even when I couldn't. This was not an easy task since, because of my illness, I left the house only once every week or two. So I surrounded myself with people who were not physically with me.

16 Thomas S. Monson, "We Never Walk Alone," *Ensign*, Nov. 2013, 124.

17 Jeffrey R. Holland, "The Ministry of Angels," *Ensign*, Nov. 2008, 30–31.

Sister Elaine S. Dalton, former Young Women's General President, unknowingly became one of my angels. She always seemed to have the perfect words of encouragement for me as I listened to her talks and devotionals online. She often testified of God's awareness of us during trying circumstances.

The prophet Enos, in the Book of Mormon, experienced his own anguish until the Savior swept away his guilt (see Enos 1:6); this taught me about my eternal potential.

Stephanie Nielson, author of the *NieNie Dialogues* blog and *Heaven is Here*, allowed me to see my own divine identity. She vividly described the search to find hers after more than eighty percent of her body was burned in an airplane crash.

The Apostle Paul wrote in an epistle to the Hebrews, "For God is not unrighteous, therefore he will not forget your work and labor of love, which ye have showed toward his name, in that ye have ministered to the saints, and do minister" (JST Hebrews 6:10). I felt peace knowing my works and testimony had been recorded by angels.

As I healed, I slowly transitioned from my scripture and online angels to others who supported me. Seven months after I had been home, I was finally feeling better enough to go on a temple trip with two friends from my young single adult (YSA) branch. While many who surrounded me showed sincere love, these friends were among the first to treat me like a returned missionary. They thought it was so cool I had studied my mission language, and one, who was preparing to go on a mission soon, asked me for advice. Often people, probably without even realizing how much hurt they caused, seemed to act like I didn't serve a mission at all because I served a short mission. I didn't want pity or praise, but I greatly appreciated my friends' genuine and uncontrived respect.

The two sister missionaries serving in my YSA branch that summer were also heaven-sent. At first I avoided them, not wanting anything to do with missions or missionaries. But gradually, I felt like Heavenly Father handpicked them to be there for me. They took me out for frozen yogurt, and we shared favorite scriptures and discussed what we could do to help others in the branch. I began to open up about my mission. Although I shared simple explanations of my journey as a missionary and getting sick, the fact that I was sharing *anything* was monumental for me. Every word I spoke quietly stung, but they simply listened and loved.

I don't think there's any way for those sisters to completely understand the impact their friendship had on me that summer. I'm sure neither of them before their missions thought that one of the people who most needed their rescuing hand would be an active twenty-three-year-old returned missionary, bishop's daughter, and BYU-Idaho graduate. They fulfilled their call as missionaries, helping me come unto Christ, by showing me that I mattered and that I was loved. They helped me realize Heavenly Father sees me as His daughter and as a real returned missionary, not just the girl who warmed up but didn't get much past the starting line.

The many people in my life who acted as angels loved me and showed me by example what our Heavenly Father saw in me. Most of the time they never realized they were doing so. Their support strengthened me beyond my own capacity and truly was a fulfillment of the Lord's promise, "I will go before your face. I will be on your right hand and on your left, and my Spirit shall be in your hearts, and mine angels round about you, to bear you up" (D&C 84:88). Their angelic love and kindness enabled me to cultivate a deeper hope in my Savior and a greater awareness of His hand in my life. Through them I felt God wrapping His love around me and giving me strength beyond my own. Their goodness and consideration were nothing short of a miracle as they acted as Christ would have done by helping to carry my burden.

Elder Holland concluded his talk by saying, "In the process of praying for those angels to attend us, may we all try to be a little more angelic ourselves—with a kind word, a strong arm, a declaration of faith and 'the covenant wherewith [we] have covenanted.'"[18]

In every situation, we have the choice to lift or to tear down other people. Most of the time, others are hurting in some way, whether we can see it or not. My illness was known to many, but not everyone's challenges are. Whether a missionary companion, friend, family member, or stranger, we have daily opportunities to choose to serve others. Sometimes, as my companion showed, our service is being kind without complaining of inconvenience.

I promise that just as Heavenly Father never once left me alone, He will never leave you alone. He will send angels. He is with us every step of the race.

18 Jeffrey R. Holland, "The Ministry of Angels," *Ensign*, Nov. 2008, 31.

APPENDIX
THE CURRANT BUSH
BY ELDER HUGH B. BROWN

You sometimes wonder whether the Lord really knows what he ought to do with you. You sometimes wonder if you know better than he does about what you ought to do and ought to become. I am wondering if I may tell you a story that I have told quite often in the Church. It is a story that is older than you are. It's a piece out of my own life, and I've told it in many stakes and missions. It has to do with an incident in my life when God showed me that he knew best.

I was living up in Canada. I had purchased a farm. It was run-down. I went out one morning and saw a currant bush. It had grown up over six feet high. It was going all to wood. There were no blossoms and no currants. I was raised on a fruit farm in Salt Lake before we went to Canada, and I knew what ought to happen to that currant bush. So I got some pruning shears and went after it, and I cut it down, and pruned it, and clipped it back until there was nothing left but a little clump of stumps. It was just coming daylight, and I thought I saw on top of each of these little stumps what appeared to be a tear, and I thought the currant bush was crying. I was kind of simpleminded (and I haven't entirely gotten over it), and I looked at it, and smiled, and said, "What are you crying about?" You know, I thought I heard that currant bush talk. And I thought I heard it say this: "How could you do this to me? I was making such wonderful growth. I was almost as big as the shade tree and the fruit tree that are inside the fence, and now you have cut me down. Every plant in the garden will look down on me, because I didn't make what I should have made. How could you do this to me? I thought you were the gardener here." That's what I thought I heard the currant bush say, and I thought it so much that I answered. I said, "Look, little currant bush, I am the gardener here, and I know what I want you to be. I didn't intend you to be a fruit tree or a shade tree. I want you to be a currant bush, and some day, little currant bush, when you are laden with fruit, you are going to say, 'Thank you, Mr. Gardener, for loving me enough to cut me down, for caring enough about me to hurt me. Thank you, Mr. Gardener.'"

Time passed. Years passed, and I found myself in England. I was in command of a cavalry unit in the Canadian Army. I had made rather rapid progress as far as promotions are concerned, and I held the rank of field officer in the British Canadian Army. And I was proud of my position. And there was an opportunity for me to become a general. I had taken all the examinations. I had the seniority. There was just one man between me and that which for ten years I had hoped to get, the office of general in the British Army. I swelled up with pride. And this one man became a casualty, and I received a telegram from London. It said: "Be in my office tomorrow morning at 10:00," signed by General Turner in charge of all Canadian forces. I called in my valet, my personal servant. I told him to polish my buttons, to brush my hat and my boots, and to make me look like a general because that is what I was going to be. He did the best he could with what he had to work on, and I went up to London. I walked smartly into the office of the General, and I saluted him smartly, and he gave me the same kind of a salute a senior officer usually gives—a sort of "Get out of the way, worm!" He said, "Sit down, Brown." Then he said, "I'm sorry I cannot make the appointment. You are entitled to it. You have passed all the examinations. You have the seniority. You've been a good officer, but I can't make the appointment. You are to return to Canada and become a training officer and a transport officer. Someone else will be made a general." That for which I had been hoping and praying for ten years suddenly slipped out of my fingers.

Then he went into the other room to answer the telephone, and I took a soldier's privilege of looking on his desk. I saw my personal history sheet. Right across the bottom of it in bold, block-type letters was written, "THIS MAN IS A MORMON." We were not very well liked in those days. When I saw that, I knew why I had not been appointed. I already held the highest rank of any Mormon in the British Army. He came back and said, "That's all, Brown." I saluted him again, but not quite as smartly. I saluted out of duty and went out. I got on the train and started back to my town, 120 miles away, with a broken heart, with bitterness in my soul. And every click of the wheels on the rails seemed to say, "You are a failure. You will be called a coward when you get home. You raised all those Mormon boys to join the army, then you sneak off home." I knew what I was going to get, and when I got to my tent, I was so bitter that I threw my cap and my saddle brown belt on the cot. I clinched my fists and I shook them at heaven. I said, "How could you do this to me, God? I have done everything I could do to measure up. There is nothing that I could have done—that I should have done—that I haven't done. How could you do this to me?" I was as bitter as gall.

And then I heard a voice, and I recognized the tone of this voice. It was my own voice, and the voice said, "I am the gardener here. I know what I want you to do." The bitterness went out of my soul, and I fell on my knees by the cot to ask forgiveness for my ungratefulness and my bitterness. While kneeling there I heard a song being sung in an adjoining tent. A number of Mormon boys met regularly every Tuesday night. I usually met with them. We would sit on the floor and have a Mutual Improvement Association. As I was kneeling there, praying for forgiveness, I heard their voices singing:

> It may not be on the mountain height or over the stormy sea;
> It may not be at the battle's front my Lord will have need of me;
> But if, by a still, small voice he calls to paths that I do not know,
> I'll answer, dear Lord, with my hand in thine:
> I'll go where you want me to go.[22]

I arose from my knees a humble man. And now, almost fifty years later, I look up to him and say, "Thank you, Mr. Gardener, for cutting me down, for loving me enough to hurt me." I see now that it was wise that I should not become a general at that time, because if I had I would have been senior officer of all western Canada, with a lifelong, handsome salary, a place to live, and a pension when I'm no good any longer, but I would have raised my six daughters and two sons in army barracks. They would no doubt have married out of the Church, and I think I would not have amounted to anything. I haven't amounted to very much as it is, but I have done better than I would have done if the Lord had let me go the way I wanted to go.

I wanted to tell you that oft-repeated story because there are many of you who are going to have some very difficult experiences: disappointment, heart-break, bereavement, defeat. You are going to be tested and tried to prove what you are made of. I just want you to know that if you don't get what you think you ought to get, remember, "God is the gardener here. He knows what he wants you to be."[23] Submit yourselves to his will. Be worthy of his blessings, and you will get his blessings.

---

22 "I'll Go Where You Want Me to Go," *Hymns*, 270.

23 Hugh B. Brown, "The Currant Bush," *New Era*, Jan. 1973 (used with permission).

ABOUT THE AUTHOR

Kristilyn grew up in Iowa City, Iowa. She graduated from Brigham Young University-Idaho, where she studied Early Childhood Education/Special Education and French, and attended the University of Utah to earn her Master of Special Education. In addition to the gospel, some of her favorite things in life are running, spending time with family and friends, traveling, and eating warm chocolate-chip cookies. Kristilyn is married to her best friend, Jeffrey. They currently reside in northern Utah with their children and their cat, Piper.